the simple guide to GARDEN PONDS

Terry Anne Barber

t.f.h.

T.F.H. Publications, Inc.

Distributed in the UNITED STATES to the Pet Trade by T.F.H. Publications, Inc., 1 TFH Plaza, Neptune City, NJ 07753; on the Internet at www.tfh.com; in CANADA by Rolf C. Hagen Inc., 3225 Sartelon St., Montreal, Quebec H4R 1E8; Pet Trade by H & L Pet Supplies Inc., 27 Kingston Crescent, Kitchener, Ontario N2B 2T6; in ENGLAND by T.F.H. Publications, PO Box 74, Havant PO9 5TT; in AUSTRALIA AND THE SOUTH PACIFIC by T.F.H. (Australia), Pty. Ltd., Box 149, Brookvale 2100 N.S.W., Australia; in NEW ZEALAND by Brooklands Aquarium Ltd., 5 McGiven Drive, New Plymouth, RD1 New Zealand; in SOUTH AFRICA by Rolf C. Hagen S.A. (PTY.) LTD., P.O. Box 201199, Durban North 4016, South Africa; in Japan by T.F.H. Publications. Published by T.F.H. Publications, Inc.

Contents

A Japanese Tradition Page 19

Convert-a-
Pond
Page 38

Toxic Foam page 57

The Real Price page 60

One Pump–
One Job
page 71

Hiding
Filters
page 81

Suck It Out!
Page 107

Chapter 11: When You Want Pondzilla 129

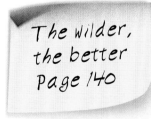

Volume
Formulas
page 120

Chapter 12: Moving the Waters 135

The wilder,
the better
Page 140

*Whew!
Ammonia!
page 146*

*Nesting
Grounds
page 167*

Toad Houses Page 203

Check the Water Company Page 223

Chapter 20: Do Your Chores

Change, Change, Change Page 230

Welcome to the fun and exciting hobby of pond-keeping. I have been a pond-keeper for many years now, and a keeper of aquarium fish for most of my life. The hobby of pond-keeping is relatively new, but its popularity is increasing at a fast pace. I can tell that just by the number of products and books that have become available over the past five years.

I have found that pond-keeping lore is spread out over many sources. In some ways this is a good thing, because it gives people like me something to do with their time, but it also is bad because finding just the right information can become a treasure hunt. I wanted to put all that stuff you need to get started into one source. Some of the information is pretty technical; some of it is not. I think there is something for you in this book.

I will do my best to explain the art and science of pond-building and-keeping, but I don't want you to walk away from the book with just a mastery of the science part. The heart and soul of the hobby is in the art. You have a complex palette of plants and animals that you will use to create your own impressionist landscape. Amidst all the technology, don't forget this hobby is fun, too!

Happy Ponding!

Terry Anne Barber

Part One

Plan Before You Dig

"Whoops! I guess the pond was supposed to be
15 feet WIDE and 4 feet DEEP"

Why Add Water to the Garden?

You probably can't wait to get started building your first pond and buying all the goodies that go into it. Before you do that, though, let's talk about the origins of the hobby and some of the joys of water gardening. I'll also explain some of the things you need to think about before you jump in.

I built my first pond on a whim. It was nice, but I wish I had done some research first. You want to be happy with your choices, so I'll point out some things you need to consider before you pick a size and style for your water garden. I'll also give you hints on how to find the right place to buy your supplies.

Even a small pond increases the beauty and diversity of your yard.

Welcome to Pond-Keeping

Welcome to a hobby that will excite you all year long: a flurry of activity in the spring as you clean up the winter detritus; the lazy days of summer as your little world blooms and flourishes; the golden days of autumn as you scoop leaves off the bottom and watch your little baby toads hop off for their long winter's nap; and finally, the bittersweet end of the season when you prepare your plants and fish for the cold days of winter ahead.

The Beauty of Water

You stroll through a beautiful garden. The sound of moving water lures you to a hidden corner. You see a small waterfall and a beautiful pool. Water lilies and lotus blossoms dazzle your eyes. Then, what was that? A fish so yellow and shiny that it must be made of gold snaps a bug off the surface of the water. You see a large rock where you can sit and gaze at this little microcosm. Frogs peer at you from under the lily pads. There are interesting plants in and around the pond. And oh, those fish! You have never seen anything like them. After a while, you realize that you feel very relaxed.

Many things went into creating this idyllic scene. Over the next 250 or so pages I will tell you what you need to do to bring this little slice of paradise into your life. Just read on, intrepid adventurer, and we will work to that final relaxing moment when you sit quietly beside your pond listening to the sounds of water.

A Growing Hobby

Have you noticed more and more supplies for the garden pond hobby at your local retail stores? Pond-keeping is growing in popularity every year. You can even join a club to share your interest with others. Fish-keeping is the second largest hobby in the United States, and pond-keeping is just fish-keeping on a grander scale; no mere guppies for you!

Decisions, Decisions

There are many reasons people decide to build a garden pond. Maybe you would like to grow spectacular water lilies, or perhaps you have just laid eyes on that koi in a neighbor's pond. Perhaps you are already an aquarist and want to take your hobby outdoors. Whatever the reason, you will surely be pleased with your project.

You will gain new expertise in this hobby. If you are a gardener, you will become a fish-keeper. You fish-keepers will now become gardeners. Ponds and plants go together–you just can't have one without the other! A garden pond is a complete ecosystem where plants and animals balance and benefit each other. For you do-it-yourself types, a world of gadgets and various projects awaits you.

More Than Your Average Flower Bed

OK, what do we know so far? A garden pond can have fish and plants, and I've hinted at some other critters, but let's get philosophical for a moment. All of nature is a complete ecosystem. What does that mean? Well, it means that every component is necessary for the survival and well-being of others. I think this is a philosophy that will serve you well as a pond-keeper. Why?

Go With the Flow
Your pond will be a little ecosystem that will grow and change with time. A valuable life lesson is at hand---learn to go with the flow. The Force is with you!

You will find that over time your pond will change. You will start with a clean body of water with a few fish and a few plants, but over months...you have built it, and they will come! I'll talk more about this later, but believe me they will come. You will have bugs and frogs and toads and perhaps some really exotic critters that you didn't expect at all. When you first see a new visitor to your pond, take a deep breath. Look at your new arrival and think about the big picture. You now have a very interesting little ecosystem right in your backyard! All is well with the world.

The Sound of Running Water

OK, I've beat all around the bush. Pond-keeping is a very relaxing hobby. In this fast-paced MTV world, it may be just what you need to unwind. The sound of running water has natural soothing effects. Place your pond in a spot where you can just sit by it and listen and observe. You won't regret it.

A Brief History of Water in the Garden

There are two traditions for water in the garden, European and Asian. Each style has its own unique approach to design. The modern water gardener can borrow from one or both, depending upon your personal tastes.

A Japanese Tradition
A water garden has traditionally been part of the Japanese garden. A stroll through the Japanese garden was meant to invoke deep relaxation and a meditative state in the visitor. One of the most memorable experiences in my life was my visit to the temples of Kyoto. I will never forget taking that very small path that beckoned me into a bamboo stand. I emerged to find a beautiful koi pond and a lovely teahouse. I enjoyed a traditional Japanese lunch, sitting cross-legged on the floor looking right out on the koi pond. On a stressful day, I can evoke that memory and really relax.

Static ornamental ponds are not the only ponds you can make today.

Japanese Approach

The art of gardening in Japan differs from the Chinese approach. Early Japanese gardens were a direct reflection of the Chinese form. However, the arrival of Zen Buddhism from China via Korea in the 6th century changed garden design in Japan. The idea of emulating nature remained, but the emphasis was on simplicity.

In Europe, gardens were an important part of large estates and the homes of the upper class. The European water gardens relied more on fountains and movement for effect. Fantastic displays of fountains go back to Roman times. A fountain was often part of the town square. You will find that the European-style pond uses geometrical shapes. Large rectangular pools and perfect circles are the norm. These pools were used to display water lilies and other plants. Fish were more utilitarian and were used for mosquito control.

In the Orient, the art of the water garden is much different. The art of pond-keeping in the Orient began in dynastic China. The prevailing philosophies of the time were Taoism and Confucianism. These philosophies emphasize humanity's integration with nature. The reflection of these ideas is apparent in Chinese art and gardening from this time period. However, the Chinese garden also emphasized other aspects of the Imperial Dynasties: wealth and power. This gives us a very interesting mix. Garden design emphasizes both natural forms and grandeur.

The royal palaces in China had gardens covering hundreds of acres. The idea was to copy the Chinese landscape in a compact form in these gardens. Forests, hills, streams, and ponds were all part of the garden. The garden became a way to display wealth in China.

Families sought to emulate the emperor and create smaller scale gardens on their property and still incorporate all of these design elements. One interesting aspect of the Chinese garden is the attempt to capture the essence of mountains with elaborate rockwork.

The Japanese perfected the art of manipulating plants and fish into forms that enhanced their natural beauty. The art of bonsai (growing miniature trees for display in the garden) is a whole book in itself. The beautiful koi or colored carp was developed in Japan to add to the enjoyment of the garden pond.

A traditional Oriental pond offers opportunities for contemplation.

Both European and Oriental traditions exist in the modern water garden. When building your own water garden, consider the merits of each and how they blend into your plans. You can mix and match ideas, depending on your taste. American water gardens are often a blend of both traditions.

Join the Club

I built my first pond ten years ago. I built it without much information and did what I thought was best based on many years of experience with aquarium-keeping. A few months later, when I had gone back to school, I met a lady in the class who had a garden pond. She put me in touch with some other people who were forming a pond club in town.

I had no idea that this relatively new hobby had such a devoted following. Not only was there a new club being formed in our town, but also it would be a chapter of a very active national club.

Koi Clubs

One of the most active clubs for pond-keepers is the Associated Koi Clubs of America (AKCA). It publishes a magazine, *Koi USA*, that is devoted to the care and showing of koi. The AKCA holds an annual seminar that features workshops on various aspects of keeping and showing koi. A judging education program is in place, and the AKCA sponsors koi shows all over the United States.

The AKCA also provides information that enables people to set up local clubs affiliated with the AKCA. The club I was in for many years was an AKCA affiliate. Some of the local clubs are bigger and more active than others. Clubs that are associated with the AKCA are not just koi-related. Most people who keep koi are also keeping plants and maybe even other types of fish in their ponds. You will find that the AKCA clubs are a good place to start if you decide the club scene is for you.

Pond Clubs

There are two other organizations that are also of interest to pond hobbyists. The National Pond Society is an organization whose goal is helping people become successful pond-keepers. They do not focus just on fish or plants, but on all aspects of the hobby. They publish a very nice magazine, conduct pond tours and classes, and appear at trade shows. They also offer a Master of Ponds certificate for people who want to really study and pass this test.

The International Water Lily Society is focused on water lilies, of course. They also publish a magazine. This is a good source of information on hybridizing lilies.

Finally, I want to tell you about another group that is more oriented to aquariums but that you might find interesting anyway. The Aquatic Gardeners Association's mission is to spread information about aquatic plants. They also study and improve the methods for growing aquatic plants in aquaria or ponds. Fellowship is a club goal. I like this because it is fun to just talk with somebody who is as enthusiastic about your hobby as you are. Have you seen that glazed-over look on someone's face when you go on and on about some new fish or plant you have? If you get into a club, you actually have somebody to talk to about this stuff who will be as thrilled as you are.

Networking

Don't forget to tell your friends about your new hobby; they may be able to hook you up with another friend who is into ponds: "That's funny, Aunt Martha also keeps goldfish."

Pond Networking

You may find that you want to get in touch with other people who are into ponds. Clubs are an excellent way to do that. There are also other ways you can share ideas about pond-keeping.

When you visit a retailer, try to get them to talk about their goods. You can learn lots of information from a good retailer. You might even find yourself admiring a fish or a plant that someone else is gazing at. Just say hello, and you may find a new pond friend.

On the Scene

What types of activities do clubs sponsor? Here's a brief description so that you can decide if you would like to join in the fun.

Koi Shows

You will see lots of blue tanks set up for a koi show. The fish will be placed in the tanks by size and class. Shows are usually decorated with colorful flags and signs and are often held at a nice public garden that you can also enjoy. You will see koi judging. It depends on the judge, but they will usually discuss why one fish wins over the others–very interesting!

Pond owners tend to band together, so put the word out.

There may be an auction where koi are sold to the highest bidder. Some koi buying and swapping takes place on the side, too. You will surely meet some folks who are very serious about koi. Many shows also have seminars during the day that cover different areas of koi-keeping. Some shows have a vendor area where you can buy fish and fish-keeping items.

Pond Tours

Pond tours are often part of the yearly meeting for the large national pond clubs. A number of people volunteer to become a stop on the pond tour, and you go from home to home admiring their ponds. Some tours use a bus, and some may just have a car caravan. Pond tours are very social events. The host will probably offer some refreshments and talk about their pond. You can ask questions, eat cookies, and make new friends.

Special Events

You will begin to learn about special events if you start subscribing to any of the pond magazines. Many of the large plant and fish farms open their facilities a few times a year. You get to tour the place, look at fish and plants, and see where your pond residents come from. One large plant seller has a festival day with vendors, a koi show, seminars, and things for sale. It can take a whole day to experience.

Become a Pond Geek

Technically, by the time you finish this book you will be a pond geek. To reach this height of geekdom, however, you need to have a computer. I am a complete computer-toting pond geek.

There are many resources waiting for you in the electronic world. Large service providers, such as CompuServe and America Online, offer forums where you can send messages to other people who like ponds. There are also usenet news groups that cater to the pond crowd. Be sure to read up on online etiquette before you post to a news group. Most of them offer a FAQ (a list of Frequently Asked Questions) that you can read to get started. It will tell you what the group's purpose is and what the rules might be. CompuServe's FishNet forum offers the most structured message area, while the usenet can be a rowdy free-for-all. Check them out and jump right in. It can be a lot of fun.

The Internet has some wonderful resources. You can find huge amounts of information. There are some great pond-related sites out there. Imagine getting a look at fish that are for sale in Japan. Maybe you cannot read Japanese, but you will see some spectacular koi on these pages.

I also want to caution you just a bit about the online world. Remember, do not share private information freely, including your address and phone number. Pond-keepers are pretty harmless people, on the whole, but you never know. If you're buying something online, take down the phone number and take care that you are using a secure server. I often find the information about products on the Internet but make purchases only over the phone.

For many, goldfish and koi are THE reason for a pond.

Before You Plunge In

There are many ways to set up your pond or water garden—more ways than you have probably thought about yet. Perhaps you have taken a recent visit to an arboretum or visited a neighbor with a backyard pond. Maybe your best friend is a duck and you don't want him to be lonely. Did you dream of owning waterfront property, and a pond is the next best thing?

Whatever your reason, let's find out if a pond is for you. You may think that all it takes is a hole and a hose. Sorry, I have a little more bad news. It won't be that easy, and I'll tell you why. The old hose and hole will quickly become a stinky algae-choked mosquito breeding ground. Not exactly lovely unless you are the Addams Family. But don't panic on me. Let's get onto the right track from the very start.

A pond lasts a long time, so plan it carefully.

Colorful koi are always welcome and certain to draw attention.

The one thing that I have learned in this hobby is you must plan, plan, and plan before you dig up even one spoonful of dirt. My first pond was pretty nice, but not adequately researched or planned. With my first pond, I made changes every step of the way until I finally got it tweaked just right. I would have saved time and money had I spent just a little time planning.

The very first thing you need to do is a little looking around. Visit your local botanical gardens for ideas. Most have a nice display of aquatic plants and lilies. Get in touch with your local water garden or pond club (yes, there probably is one; check with one of the major clubs or see the listings in a pond magazine). See if they have any pond tours coming up.

You can also visit your local plant nursery. Many nurseries and garden shops now carry a few items for the pond. You can look around and get a feel for the types of plants you like.

Also, don't forget the fish—my favorites. Yes, right now I will admit it; I am in this hobby for the fish. Go to a few aquarium stores and check out their wares. After all, you are about to create a giant aquarium. Look over the fish that are suitable for life in a pond. What do you like? OK, now forget about those piranhas for your mother-in-law's next visit. It is possible that you will not see many pond fish, or the ones you see are just ugly. Most retailers won't have the really good fish, but remember you just want to get a feel for what these guys look like.

Next stop is the library or bookstore. Look at the gardening section for books on ponds. Also look for books on fish for ponds. Some garden books have ideas for placing water features in the garden.

Your choice of fish and plants will start to define the type of pond you will need to make a good home for them. Even if you should have an idea firmly in mind, I am going to discuss the many things you should consider before you make your final decision. Maybe you will get some new ideas for your first pond or even for your second pond. This hobby is habit-forming, and once you get into it chances are that you will use water in your garden in many interesting ways.

Size Does Matter

The very first thing that you need to decide is how big your pond is going to be. You may have a very small pond in mind, or even something very large. If you plan to keep koi, you will need a larger pond than you probably expect. If you cannot build a large pond, you can keep many nice fish that will not grow as big. Also, remember to scale the size of your water plants to your new pond. Some water plants are very large and would overpower a small pond. The cool thing is that there are miniature varieties of some of the most popular pond plants, so you can tailor your plants to your new pond.

Now, if big is what you have got to have, planning is even more important. I will talk some more about this later. Just plan on a big budget to go with your big pond. You will need heavy equipment for digging, and you may want to bring in a professional water garden landscape artist.

So down to earth we come. Please consider a small pond for your first project. You want to have fun while you learn your new hobby, and this is easier with a smaller project. At the same time, too small and you will need to take some extra effort to be content with your pond.

So where does that leave us? I would say you would want to aim for something that will be 300 to 1000 gallons. Does that sound like a lot of water? It isn't really. Your bathtub holds about 80 gallons of water.

Big, elaborate ponds cost money and may be very complicated to build.

Too Big?

For a first pond, big is much harder to manage. Everything that you will need is bigger. Every bit of work will be bigger. There will be a limit to the size of hole that you can dig by hand. Don't take on more than you can manage without throwing out your back.

Even a small pond should not look sterile and fixed.

Start Small

What if you decide that the hobby is really not for you after all of your best efforts? It is going to be very difficult to remove that large cement-lined pond from your yard. I have seen quite a few former ponds filled with dirt and turned into flower beds. Frankly, that is pretty sad for me, because the pond is much more interesting. So don't overwhelm yourself; start small and you're less likely to end up with more than you can manage.

Why Your First Pond Should be Small

If you are like me, you are going to take your first pond on as a do-it-yourself project. Therefore, a small pond is probably best for your first time out. But why? Let's break it out.

First, the budget for your project will be directly proportional to the size of your pond. Pond liners are sold by the foot. Concrete is purchased by the yard. Filter systems are larger for large ponds—yup, that means more money. Unless you live next door to a football team, heavy equipment may be needed to prepare your site for a large pond.

Second, you can keep some very nice fish and plants in a small pond. The exception to the smaller is better rule regards koi. A koi can easily grow to over 24 inches long and 6 to 8 inches in diameter. That is a big fish! Big fish need lots of water to have a happy, healthy life. If you must have koi, begin to think about a larger pond or reconsider your fish choice. There really are some very nice fish for the beginner that won't get so large. I advise that you learn fish-keeping with less expensive fish. Make your second pond the one that will be home to a prize koi.

Special Safety Issues

Safety is such an important topic that it needs to be right here, front and center. I will point out safety issues as we go along, but there are a few that you should think about when planning your pond.

Electricity and Water Don't Mix

Everybody knows that it is unsafe to mix water and electricity. Water is a very good electrical conductor. When you stand in a puddle you give the current a direct path to the ground, right through you! There is enough juice in household current to kill.

There are building codes specific to areas of the home where water and electricity can come into contact. For example, it is now code in most places to have a Ground Fault Interruption Circuit (GFIC) in bathrooms and garages. A GFIC is a simple device that can save your life. In your household wiring, electricity flows into an appliance and back out again. The GFIC has its own little circuit that measures the current going out and coming back. If there is a failure to ground (in other words, the electricity doesn't come back), it shuts off the circuit. No more current. This means that if you were standing in your pond making a mai-tai and dropped the blender, you would be alive to tell about it. However, making mai-tais while standing knee-deep in water is definitely not recommended, even with a GFIC.

GFICs can be purchased in many forms. The least expensive and most readily available is a replacement for your household electrical plug. It has a little red button for testing and also a reset button. It is a very good idea to test the circuit occasionally to make sure it is working. You just push the red button and it should turn off the socket. A good time to test is just before you plan to work around your pond.

GFICs can also be purchased as part of an extension cord. These are a little more expensive but are well worth the cost. Many folks have an extension cord running out to their pond, and this is a great way to get your GFIC. Most home improvement stores will carry both types of GFICs.

This is serious business. There are also building codes regarding the proximity of electrical outlets to swimming pools. A distance of 15 feet from the pool is required by building codes in most states. Please check up on your local building codes. Use swimming pools as your guidelines and please be safe.

Clubs

Garden clubs and koi clubs are excellent sources for information on water gardens. They may even have local pond activities that you can participate in.

Any electrical fittings near the pond must be fully waterproofed.

Part 1

Electricity and water don't mix, so hire a professional if you have any doubts.

Don't Drown Your Friends

Any open water, even if it's very shallow or in very small containers, is a drowning hazard. When you design your pond, take this into consideration right from the beginning. If you have small children or your neighbors have small children, really be careful.

It is estimated that as many as 500 children under the age of 5 drown in swimming pools every year. It's a real tragedy. The very best way to prevent accidents is to put a childproof barrier around open water. Fence the little guys out and make sure you know what the kids are up to when they are outside.

The neighborhood kids and your guest's children will also be very curious about your pond. The very first thing they will do is pick up a big handful of dirt and rocks and toss it in, before you can even make a move. After you have restrained yourself from tossing the kid in with the new decorations, be sure your little guests are safe.

I had a neighbor who decided that I had built my pond for the enjoyment of her Labrador Retriever. They incorporated a swim in my koi pond into their daily walk, until I put the kibosh on that activity. While dog immersion is not a big problem for the dog or the koi, my main concern was the dog's nails puncturing the pond liner.

Local Ordinances

While we are on the topic, the local authorities may have a few rules about open water in residential areas. Imagine a knock on the door and a notice from the local authorities to remove your water garden. Don't laugh, it has happened. You may find that there are no current guidelines, or there may be regulations regarding fences. Whatever the rules, plan to follow them and to keep your family and friends safe.

Don't Forget the Animals

There can be problems with animals becoming trapped in a pond and drowning. I actually performed mouth-to-beak on four little fledgling sparrows that fell into a kiddie pool and could not climb the slippery sides. After a few puffs they started to revive and sat on the rail of the deck until they were dry and recuperated enough to fly away. All four flew away, lucky little birds. Most ponds have rockwork on the edges that should allow any small critters to climb out.

I will talk about unwanted visitors later. However, my philosophy is to not harm any pond visitors, human or animal.

Dollars and Sense—Budget Your Project

The worst thing you can do is build a garden pond on a whim. You will enjoy it much more if you just plan a little. The first thing to plan is your budget. Make sure you know what you will need and what it will cost. If you skip purchasing essential items, you can end up with a bad outcome and walk away from your pond aggravated with the experience.

One rule that you can count on is that the larger the pond, the more money you will spend. That means that the size of your budget will have everything to do with the size of your new water garden. I think it is worthwhile to save up for some of the more expensive items for the pond that will increase your enjoyment. A good pump, filter, and even an ultraviolet clarifier are important accessories.

Please don't think you need a lot of money to enjoy water gardening. Of course, the most spectacular water gardens will be large and have expensive fish swimming about. A nice ceramic pot with a lotus or lily is a stunning addition to any garden and is in everybody's budget. Some of the most creative water gardens I have seen are small. The small water garden is an unexpected treat in any landscape.

Make a List

Start by making a list. It is easy, it will keep you organized, and it will help you establish your budget. I will go over all of the items you will need for your pond during the course of this book. Here is a sneak peek to get you started on your project list. Prices given are just examples in my area, so don't use them for your numbers. Shop around and look for the best price on the items that you wish to buy. Don't let the prices in this list scare you.

How Many Gallons?

You can calculate the number of gallons a pond will hold using this simple formula: length x width x depth (all in feet) x 7.5. (The first part of this formula gives you cubic feet of volume, and there are 7.5 gallons per cubic foot.) For a pond with curved sides, just estimate the best rectangle that fits around it and subtract about 10 percent. This is all you need for a rough estimate.

This hypothetical project includes a very large liner pond with top-of-the-line items specified. It's nice to dream!

The main thing is to take some time, sit down, and think about your new water garden. Do some sketches, think about the size, and think about your budget. I always surprise myself with how much money I end up spending on odds and ends I never thought about.

Pond Planning Checklist

Construction labor: 1 day @ $500/day	$500
Pond liner: 1000 sq. ft.	$600
Rock: 10 tons @ $15/ton	$150
Filter: 1	$400
UV Clarifier: 1	$150
Pump: 1	$150
Plumbing: Misc. hardware	$300
Plants: 12 @ $20	$240
Fish: 12 feeders @ $1	$12
Total	$2502

Planning Your First Pond

Congratulations! You are on the way to your first water garden. Please keep reading and you can avoid many of the mistakes first-timers often make. My first pond was a 1,000-gallon liner pond. I did very little research and plunged ahead anyway. I think it turned out pretty well, but there were many, many things that needed to be fixed as time went on—little mistakes here and there. Things I just didn't think about provided me with hours of weekend projects to get it just right. I really do like to tinker with things, but this was too much.

So, after the fact, I joined a pond club. I also bought a few books and started to find easier ways around these things. But I know that you won't have any problems—well, maybe you will tinker around a little,

Will your pond feature plants, fish, or both?

Container gardens may be your best bet if you lack land and time.

Heavy Water

Water is heavy. Remember the old saying, "A pint's a pound"? A gallon of water weighs 8.3 pounds—that's 83 pounds for a 10-gallon container! Take the weight into account when placing your container pond on a deck or balcony.

but let's make it fun. I just received an e-mail from a person admiring me for my fortitude in pond-keeping. It's too bad that this person has a 1,000-gallon pond and they don't really like it. It doesn't take fortitude, just some planning.

More About Size

You already know that each size pond will have its own rewards and challenges. Just for convenience, let's talk about ponds in three general sizes: small, medium, and large. These size categories are a little arbitrary, so if your pond falls somewhere between that's all right. Take a look at each section. It will help you decide what will be right for you.

Container Gardens

These are the small to really small ponds. The beauty of these small gardens is that you can integrate one or many into your landscape. A container garden is also ideal for an apartment or small home where you may only have a small patio. Your creativity is the limit for these little gardens. Anything that can hold water can be incorporated into your garden.

Let's just say that anything under 100 gallons is a container garden. A container that has less than 5 gallons is really too small. Five gallons is about the size of a household mopping bucket, and 100 gallons is roughly a bathtub full. Small ponds are easy to keep–you just complete a few little chores each week.

Look for a container that is at least 12 inches deep. If you can find something that is a little deeper, say 18 inches, that would be better. You will need a little depth if you plan to keep water lilies or any fish. Water lilies need 6 to 12 inches of water above their crown to grow well. Fish need a little depth for swimming and for keeping cool.

Changing the water is the single best thing you can do for these little ponds. For a very small container, say 5 to 20 gallons, plan on changing one-quarter to one-half of the water volume each week. For larger gardens, 20 to 100 gallons, one-tenth to one-quarter per week is plenty. Water changes alone will eliminate a whole host of potential problems.

Siphon It!

If you can't install a drain, a siphon is an excellent way to drain your container garden or small pond. You can make a siphon out of an old piece of garden hose or clear tubing purchased from a home supply store. Get a piece that is at least half an inch in diameter or the job will just take too long.

Have you ever started a siphon? Just place one end in your water garden and suck on the other end. Gak! Pond water! Here is a better way. Immerse the whole length of tube in the water. Block off one end with a finger, then take the blocked end out of the water. Place the tube into your waste bucket and unblock the end. Remember, this won't work unless the waste bucket is lower than what you are draining.

You can also purchase a siphon rig from your local aquarium or pet retailer. Look for a complete setup that has a hose long enough to reach your water garden. There are some major advantages to using these aquarium gizmos. The siphon uses the flowing water at your tap to suck up the water from your pond. It also has an attachment to help you suck up any muck from the bottom of the container. The wastewater conveniently goes down your drain, too–no lugging buckets of pond water through the living room from your balcony.

Bring Me My Bucket!

A half whiskey barrel is a popular small container. Whiskey barrel gardens look great where you have a country style garden. Your local garden shop may carry them as planters. You can either purchase or make a liner for the barrel so it will hold the water. I have seen pre-formed liners made specifically for half whiskey barrels. If you make your own liner, use a pond-grade material to prevent leaks. I recommend PVC for this application because it is thin enough to easily form into a small container.

Ceramic crocks come in many shapes and sizes. Select one that is large enough to hold 10 gallons of water or more. Most will already be glazed and water-tight. An unglazed crock

Drain, Drain, Drain

When you pick your container, look for one to which you can add a bottom drain. Also, be sure that you have a convenient place to drain the water. The neighbors on the patio below may not enjoy the 20-gallon shower you plan for them each week.

will weep water. Look for one that is glazed on the inside at the very least. No liner will be needed. If you must have an unglazed crock, use a PVC liner. You can attach the top edges of the liner to the inside of the crock with aquarium-grade silicone sealer.

Another way to seal a ceramic container is to coat the inside of the pot with two layers of polyurethane. Use either the type that you spray on or brush on. This polyurethane will be available at a home improvement center or paint store. After the polyurethane has completely dried, wash it well before you add anything to your pond.

Make Mine a Medium

Now we are starting to talk about some water! Midsize ponds are the 100- to 800-gallon variety. Most of you will probably want to build a pond in this range for your first pond. You can do most of the work with common garden tools and your own muscle. Hold off on joining the gym, though, as there are ways to build a nice midsize pond without extensive digging. A size medium with no digging has some real advantages besides

A PVC liner makes a half whiskey barrel into a container garden.

Other Sources

Try going to an antique store, flea market, or junkyard for items that can be used to make an unusual container garden. You can come up with some unique items that can add a whimsical touch to your garden. Armed with a PVC liner and some silicone sealer, the sky is the limit.

bypassing the sore muscles. You will have the option of moving the pond or making changes without having to dig new areas of your yard. This is a good way to make sure the hobby is for you.

Plastic Puddles

Garden ponds have become more popular, and there are many pre-formed plastic ponds now available. You will probably see them at your local home supply store or garden center. They range in size from less than 100 gallons to a few hundred gallons.

Look for a container that has some depth to it; some of these small containers are very shallow. If your pond is not at least 12 to 18 inches deep you may have a few problems. First, water lilies need some depth to grow properly. Second, if you live in a northern climate, a shallow pond will definitely freeze solid in the winter. Your fish and plants will not appreciate being made into pondsicles! You can use a shallow pond if you live in a warm climate or if you plan to bring your fish in for the winter. Many pond-keepers do this, but it complicates your life a little.

You can use several of these pre-formed ponds to build a series of ponds that are connected. Some of these systems have plastic waterfalls that you can incorporate into your pond. I personally don't think a plastic waterfall looks very good without some extra work to add rocks so it looks more natural, but that's a matter of taste.

Move Over

Stock tanks are large containers used to provide water for cows and horses. What is really cool about these containers is that they are deep, big, and relatively low-priced. I really like stock tanks as garden ponds.

Most stock tanks have a number of features that make them ideal for small ponds. They are made of a tough plastic and are much

Pre-formed ponds offer an excellent start in the hobby.

thicker than pre-formed plastic pond containers. They are an attractive dark gray. The only thing you may not like about them is their shape. Stock ponds come in round, oblong, or square—not very natural-looking.

King-sized Projects

Most suburban gardeners will not want to go for the truly large pond, but there are definitely times when a large pond is preferred. Most people who keep show koi like a large pond. These fish require lots of room to grow to their potential—we are talking about fish that reach over 24 inches in length! Remember that big fish mean big water. Let's talk about a few ways to build a really big pond.

Natural Ponds

You may have a stream or spring on your land that you can use to fill an earth-bottomed pond. You can build some really spectacular water gardens using natural water like this, but most such projects are large and expensive. It would be a very special project. My recommendation for you here is to seek out the advice of an expert and also consider having a professional build your pond. Some of the most beautiful projects I have seen were earth-bottomed ponds using a natural water source to fill them.

Large Liner Ponds

You can use liners to line as big a hole as you want to dig. Heavy equipment is recommended, and just think about where you would put all that dirt.

If you decide on a truly huge liner pond, a careful survey of your site for elevations is a good idea. You may wish to contract with a professional for such a large project. You will likely need large amounts of rock to make your pond look natural, too.

Pond liners are sold by the square foot and can be joined to form large liners. Liners are used in landfills to contain the liquid that leaches from the buried garbage. (Charming thought, isn't it?) The point is, there are sources for large liners. Just make sure what you use is safe for fish.

Convert-a-Pond

If you already have a natural pond on your property, you may just want to spruce things up a bit or add a few fish. Be careful with the types of water plants you add. Many are incredibly invasive and could quickly take over the entire pond. Take the time to visit a water lily grower just to see how invasive these plants can be.

Part 1

Convert That Old Swimming Pool

I have seen this done and it really looks great. If you get sick of the constant skimming and chemicals, just convert your pool into a fishpond. You may be able to use some of the equipment you already have for your swimming pool. However, swimming pool filters don't work very well for fishponds. The volume of particles in a fishpond quickly plugs up a swimming pool filter, making it practically useless.

A large, deep pond like an old swimming pool is an ideal home for koi. Koi do really well when they can swim in deep water. The disadvantage is that it may be too deep for many water plants. You would have to construct shelves and pedestals to raise your lilies to the correct depth. Wow, just imagine some simulated Greek columns supporting water lilies with big koi cruising down to the depths. It could be spectacular.

A small formal concrete pond with containers.

What Lives In a Pond?

You have considered what size pond or water garden to build, now think about what kind of critters you would like to populate your little aquatic world. Plants and animals work together to make a complete ecosystem. Each benefits from the other. Keeping both plants and fish makes your water garden more complete.

My pond philosophy is to make a home for a variety of plants and animals so that the pond develops into a complete ecosystem. Plants benefit from animals, animals benefit from plants. But for some water-gardens, it can complicate matters, too. Let's review the pros and cons of keeping different living things in your pond so that you can plan for your ideal situation.

Concrete Ponds

The techniques are about the same as needed in concrete swimming pool construction. You would have a very permanent structure to house your plants and fish. Concrete construction is the most expensive way to go, but the results can be really stunning. Concrete can be used to make rounded shapes and construct plant shelves. For a really large project, again you may wish to contact a professional for help.

Water lilies probably are the most commonly used pond plants.

Though not beautiful, oxygenating plants are useful in any pond.

Just Wet Salad

It is perfectly fine to keep only plants in your new pond. The smaller your pond, the more difficult it will be to keep fish. In a container garden it makes perfect sense not to keep fish, though I think a fish or two adds to a container garden.

There are many types of aquatic plants that you can keep in your new pond. Each has its own special requirements, but all are easy. Aquatic plants are hardy and are really no problem for folks with basic gardening skills. In fact, some plants will become more like an alien being, trying to take over the world. You will end up tossing the stuff out as fast as it grows.

Many water plants have been hybridized and developed for water gardeners. Others have not been so tamed and are just like their wild counterparts. Water lilies and lotus have been cultivated for many decades and are available in many colors, sizes, and shapes. There are catalogs that are put out by many of the lily hybridizers, and you will be able to find some really special plants only through these catalogs. In fact, catalogs are a good source for most water plants. Just be sure to follow the planting instructions that come with your new plants.

Add Some Fish

Fish add interest and color to your pond. I like to watch fish. They dart around, eat bugs, eat from your hand, and play all sorts of fishy games. The main reason to add fish to your pond is for mosquito control. Your new pond will draw breeding mosquitoes to lay their eggs and grow their larvae. It just won't be fun to sit by your pond and be attacked by the nasty little vampires. Good news: This is a very easy problem to solve. Many fish love to eat mosquito larvae.

Goldfish varieties are the most popular and common as pond fish. They come in many shapes and sizes, plain and fancy. Many goldfish and carp types have been bred for centuries to meet certain beauty standards, like breeds of dogs, to please the eye. I will talk about the common and not-so-common types of fish that can be kept in a pond later.

Your success with fish-keeping will depend upon your commitment. Just remember they are animals that deserve a nice life. There are some common fallacies about fish that just aren't true. Let's go over a few.

Many myths have grown up about keeping fish, even just goldfish.

"Fish Don't Live Very Long"

Oh, not true! Fish can have very long lives. Many ocean-going species can live for decades. Fish kept in home aquaria have a natural life span as long as 10 years, and pond fish can have some of the longest lives. Koi are especially long-lived, with reports of life spans up to 100 years! A properly kept fish will give you years of enjoyment.

"Fish Can Just Be Flushed Down the Toilet"

I wonder if the person who started this one thought about it much. Flushing a fish condemns it to a slow death. They don't somehow magically go to freedom when you flush them. The fish will starve or die of suffocation or cold, slowly.

"Fish Don't Feel Pain"

Fish have a simple nervous system, but experiments have shown that fish react to pain stimuli. I pity the poor fish that volunteered for

Joys of Spring

I will never forget the night of a thousand toads. One spring night the racket outside at the pond was just deafening. I was used to a few peepers here and there, but this was an all-out assault on the ears. I went out to see what the fuss was, and there must have been a thousand toads! Each male toad was singing his little heart out to attract a mate. I won't say what else was going on in the pond, because this is a family book.

Treefrogs may be one of the first "critters" to find your pond.

Possums also may find your pond, but they do little damage.

that experiment. Sadly, there are times when it may be best to quickly dispatch a sick fish.

Properly cared for, your fish and its offspring will reward you with many hours of enjoyment. Treat them as kindly as you would any family pet.

Critters You Didn't Expect

This is the fun part. Your pond will become the home or stopping place for a variety of animals. Frogs will come to stay. Toads will visit in the spring. Birds will stop for a bath or a drink of water. Some animals may come in search of a snack. The bugs will find all sorts of things to do in your pond. This will be *fun*, really. Think of it as your own little science project.

You may also have a few unwelcome visitors that come to make a snack of your pond inhabitants. This is when it is time to be philosophical. If you live in a suburb, you will be amazed by the number of animals that find ways to live with us. Raccoons, skunks, and possums are common and may come to visit your water. If you are in a rural area, you may see some more exotic specimens. Wonderful, isn't it? I have decided to keep some fish that are cheap, reproduce well, and are no great loss should they become some animal's lunch. There's no point in harming the local wildlife; just learn to live with them.

Finding Your Supplies

It would really be nice if you could do one-stop shopping with this hobby, but this is very unlikely. That's why it's important to distinguish the gems from the clinkers as you hop from store to store. Some of you may live in more remote areas, like me. Take heart–you will soon discover the joys of catalog shopping, but you also may need to take some road trips to find just the right things for your pond. Traveling has been one of the fun parts of the hobby for me. I love going to koi shows, lily farms, and garden shops to look for a new fish or plant.

The good news is that pond-keeping is becoming more and more popular. As the demand grows, more retailers are carrying items for the pond

Not everything you need for your pond will be available locally.

hobby. I started pond-keeping about ten years ago, and in this short amount of time I have seen more items offered for sale every year to make pond-keeping fun and convenient.

So what is an eager pondologist to do? Where can you go for supplies for your new hobby?

What to Avoid

First, you don't have to settle for limp plants, dead fish, and stinky water. If the plants are sickly, the water is smelly, and the fish look nasty, take your hard-earned dollars somewhere else. Of course, it is a matter of degree, but if a place looks shabby, it is. Imagine buying a plant that just continues to wither despite your best efforts, or worse, bringing home a diseased fish to infect your whole pond. Disaster!

However, a new pond-keeper may see some situations that look bad but really aren't. For example, a water plant display at a dealer that has green pea soup water is not necessarily bad. The grower has probably recently fertilized the water plants and the algae are having a field day. Are the plants nice and green, with new growth evident? If yes, you are probably looking at some good stuff.

You want to avoid the cheap stuff, as well. Buy the best quality items that your budget will allow. This applies not only to fish and plants, but to pond hardware too. Some items may be inexpensive to purchase but will wear out quickly and cost you more in the long run. I will point out these potential problems when I discuss each hardware item. Since you are new to this, however, it'll be more difficult at first to determine the best names in hardware.

Ponds, Not Food Gardens

There are a few water plants that are edible, like watercress. Be careful when eating plants from your pond, as there are cases of humans contracting parasites from eating water plants. They're rare, but it doesn't hurt to be careful. If you want to grow water plants for food, grow them in a special container, away from any fish.

Water Plants

Many nurseries now carry a small selection of water plants. First look at the overall appearance of the plant. Does it have many dead and dying leaves? A few dead or dying leaves may be normal for many water plants, because they shed the old leaves and grow new ones. But any dealer worth their salt will take the time to properly prune the plants and remove dying leaves. If the plant has a few not-so-good leaves and lots of new growth, it's probably in good shape.

Lilies

Water lilies are available in a huge array of leaf colors and bloom colors. There are day-bloomers and night-bloomers. Water lilies and lotus have been hybridized to give a truly fabulous array of varieties for every water garden.

Next, lift the plant out of the water. Inspect the container it is in. Does it look over-crowded, like it's exploding from the pot? This isn't bad either, but plan on repotting this plant when you get it home. Is there enough potting material in the pot? Don't be alarmed if the plant is only potted in gravel. This is OK, although it's not my preferred potting method.

A well-balanced pond will have several types of aquatic plants. Let's talk about the four main types.

Oxygenators

This category of plants will add oxygen to your pond. They are the plants that you probably think of as pond weeds. They look very delicate and feathery and actually require no pot, but you can also pot them to keep them from floating all over the pond. Oxygenators are really lovely to view from above and make great fish food, too. Koi-keepers will have a hard time keeping these in the pond, as the koi will eat every sprig.

Submerged Plants

These are the plants that normally grow in the mud at the bottom of lakes and ponds. You will plant these in pots

Bunch plants such as Myriophyllum are easy to find locally.

Spatterdock, Nuphar, produces a beautiful yellow flower like a water lily.

and submerge them to the proper depth for best growth. Water lilies, lotus, and spatterdock are the most common types. These plants are the most lovely of all pond plants.

Marginals

Marginal describes the favored growing place for these plants–on the edges of the water. There are many plants that fall into this class. Marginal plants add interesting foliage, blooms, and textures to your pond. They are very easy to keep.

Shelves

Most people build a shelf on one side of their pond where they can set pots of marginals. As you progress with your project, go ahead and plan for a place to keep marginal plants.

When you plan your pond, remember to set aside an area to display marginal plants. They will just barely have their pots under the surface of the water. I have kept some marginals with the lips of the pots out of the water to discourage foraging koi. You will need to water their pots if they become dry. Just punch a hole in the bottom and you will be all set.

Water lettuce, Pistia, rapidly covers a pond in a warm climate.

Floaters

Floating plants can play an essential role in your pond. They help to keep the surface covered to keep fish cool in the summer and also perform an amazing amount of natural filtration for the pond. Many grow like something from a science fiction movie. Take heart–they also make great compost.

Gone Fishin'

Finding good quality pond fish is a little harder than finding good plants. Your success will largely depend on the popularity of the hobby in your area. I have had the hardest time finding really good pond fish. I know where to go for the really expensive koi, but nice common goldfish are more elusive.

You want to only buy fish that look healthy, happy, and bright. How do you tell? The fish should not be hanging around on the sides or bottom of its tank. It should not have any damage to its fins or scales. If there is a dead fish in the vat, pass on the whole lot of them.

It is customary when buying koi to ask the seller to place the fish in a small container so that you can examine the fish more closely. You will look for health and the conformation of the fish. Regardless of type, a good look to see that the fish is healthy is always a good idea.

So let's forge ahead and talk about where to get your stuff.

Where to Go

Finding your pond supplies can make you into a treasure seeker. Let's discuss the pros and cons of each place to buy your supplies. I'm going to give you my general opinion of each outlet, but remember that there will be good ones and bad ones in each category. Use your best shopping skills to find the best quality for the money.

Shops

Pet stores are one place to look for fish and some plants. Even in a pet store that sells all kinds of things, the fish department can make up a large percentage of sales. You may get lucky and find members of the staff who know fish. There are different types of pet stores to consider.

Mom-and-pops are the small neighborhood pet stores. They will usually carry supplies that appeal to the interests of the owner. You are in luck, though. The aquarium hobby is large and you are bound to find a mom-and-pop that caters to the fish crowd. The bad news is that pond fish may not make up a large percentage of their business. Still, look over the coldwater species they offer. You will probably see fancy goldfish. They are pretty but may not be the hardiest of pond inhabitants. Don't forget to look at the tropical fish, too. If you live in a warm climate or are willing to keep your fish in an aquarium for the winter, there are tropical species that could make really nice pond fish.

Special Order
Another point about mom-and-pops: They will probably be willing to special order items for you. These will be the most flexible dealers you will find. If you find a good local small retailer, you have found gold.

Here is my favorite trick. Ask to look at the feeder fish. These are the ones destined to become food for other critters. Guess what? They can make great pond fish. The big problem is that feeders are usually kept in very crowded conditions, and you may see dead and dying fish in their tank, which is not good. If you see a feeder tank where the population looks relatively healthy, this is a source for some really nice and really cheap pond fish. You usually buy feeders at a dozen or so for a dollar. Not bad!

For plants, mom-and pops will likely carry some plants for tropical aquaria. The only plants you may be interested in here are the oxygenators. You may even end up bringing some back to your retailer for trade. You shouldn't expect to find any really unusual plants at a mom-and-pop, but you can often find a truly amazing array of aquarium "standards." Many of these will make great pond plants.

Pet superstores work on relatively low margins and need to move inventory quickly and inexpensively. Livestock is a costly item for them, and most offer only a small selection of fish for sale. Your experience will probably depend on the expertise of the store's staff. I buy fish from these outlets because my choice is a little limited in my geographic area, but I know that I absolutely *must* quarantine these fish, expect to lose a few, and nurse them back to health before they can ever enter my pond.

Home and garden stores will offer decent prices on many pond items. You will also find lots of items for landscaping your pond. I love to shop in these stores for tubing, piping, and other plumbing-related items that can be used in pond-building. I like to save money by building a few things myself, too, and I get the parts here. Get creative and browse the store. Plastic tubs and plumbing connectors are useful for many do-it-yourself pond projects. Your imagination is the limit in a store like this.

Mail Order

If you live in a rural area, you will discover the joys of mail order shopping. There is a wide variety of possibilities for shopping by catalog for the pond hobby.

Healthy feeder goldfish often grow into big, colorful, inexpensive pond joys.

A few of the established garden supply catalogs are beginning to offer pond items. They may also offer garden items that you would like to use around your pond, such as statues. I have been pleasantly surprised with the items for ponds showing up lately in this type of catalog.

Credit Card It!
When buying from a catalog, using a credit card is very wise. If you are not happy with the purchase, you can dispute the charge on your card.

You will also find specialty catalogs. There are several companies that offer water lilies as their specialty. You will find species of water plants here that you may not find anywhere else. You will likely receive bare root specimens; this means the plant arrives in a baggie with no dirt, no pot. This is OK, but these plants require some tender loving care (TLC) to reach their full potential. Many may not bloom the first season, as they will be expending their energy to form new roots and leaves. Take heart: next year you will be rewarded with truly lovely and unique specimens.

There are also a few specialty catalogs that carry pond hardware–pumps, filters, liners, and other accessories. This is a great way to buy. You will likely find some of the best prices available. The problem is that you will need to know more about the items you want, but many catalog outlets have a phone staff available to answer questions. (Just remember they want to sell you something.) Reputable dealers will take returns if you find that the item you purchased is not exactly what you wanted.

Collecting Your Own Specimens

I've collected a few water lilies and oxygenating plants myself, but I want to caution you that collecting wild specimens may be illegal in some areas. There are also plants that cannot be transported across state lines because some water plants can become so noxious that they clog waterways and ponds. Others may be rare and protected. Be careful.

The plant you collect may also be unable to tolerate the much warmer water it will find in your pond. This will be especially true of any plant or animal removed from a stream. If you collect wild specimens, make sure that they can survive the conditions in your pond.

Wild water lilies are very hardy, but it will be difficult to find any with other than white

Water lilies usually are planted in baskets to control their spread.

blooms. To dig a wild lily, gently lift the tubers out of the mud. You may break the tubers free, but you must collect a growing "corm" on the bulb. This is the part of the plant that produces the leaves and blooms. Like a bare-root specimen, the plant may be a little shocky after its move and require a season of TLC to do well for you.

Make a rule to disturb the habitat as little as possible. Root around as little as you can get away with to remove only one or two bulbs. You will also have to muck about in some really gooey mud beds. Most likely, you can bypass the leeches and get a better specimen at your local nursery.

Part Two
Equipment

"I'm telling you, sir, the resolution on your garden pond will be sooooo much higher when you get a satellite."

Keep That Water Clean: Filters

You want to be able to admire your beautiful plants and fish, but you won't be able to see them if you don't invest in some equipment to keep your water sparkling clear and clean. Take a deep breath and get ready to dig into the nitty gritty of pond equipment. There are many facts to consider and even some calculations to do so that you can choose the best equipment for your pond.

Not only do you have to choose the right equipment, but you need to know how to put it all together. I'm talking about plumbing. I will give you some pointers and ideas on how to assemble your equipment so that it does the job and looks nice, too.

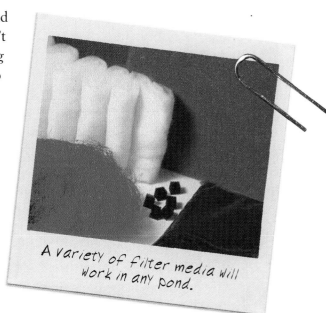

A variety of filter media will work in any pond.

Natural Ponds

Some people like to run what is called a natural pond. They work very hard to balance the plants and fish to eliminate the need for filtration. The real key to this is to keep very few fish. Personally, fish are the major reason I keep a pond, so filter system here I come.

Filtration Basics

To filter or not to filter? That is the question for most pond-keepers. The point can be debated endlessly, but if you want to keep a large number of small fish or a small number of large fish, you need a filter. Now you need to decide what type of filter you want and how large it must be.

If you have no fish, you can go without. You could also go without in a container garden. If you have a fish or two in your container garden, frequent water changes can take the place of a filter.

You will hear a lot about filters when you get into this hobby. There are filter fads in pond circles, and everybody will rave about the latest filter gadget that will solve all of your pond problems. However, most filters are different twists on the same theme, so let's go over the basics first, then delve into some filter intricacies.

There are three types of filtration that can be used for ponds. Your best choice will probably incorporate one or more methods to make a complete system. The three types are:

√ Mechanical filtration

√ Biological filtration

√ Chemical filtration.

Mechanical Filtration

Mechanical filtration is simply the removal of solid materials from a fluid. The solids may be so small that you cannot see them with the naked eye. You would simply be amazed at the different products that are filtered to remove particles. From the plastic that makes sandwich bags to the medicines injected into your body, all are filtered to remove particles.

Mulm

Mulm is the brown substance that collects in the bottom of ponds and fish tanks. It is made up of fish wastes and other large organic materials, such as dead algae.

OK, back to ponds. Let's face it, there is going to be a lot of solid material that will best be removed from your pond. You will have large materials like leaves and bits of plants and smaller solids like fish poop. You will also have very small particles that will make up much of the solids in your pond. Algae and other small living things will be heavily represented in the solid material.

The problem with trying to remove these small particles is that there are just so darned many of them, billions and billions, to be exact. Most mechanical filters are just some sort of screen that keeps the particles from going through, so to catch very small particles you need very tiny holes in the screen. The particles of course will clog up filters as they get trapped in the tiny holes in a filter. Trying to remove very small particles just won't be very effective. If you can find a tight enough filter, it will clog so fast that it is nearly useless.

Prefilters help eliminate leaves and other large bits of trash.

Biological Filtration

There will also be dissolved wastes in your pond. These are small molecules that are primarily the product of fish life. Let's face it: A fish is swimming around in its own toilet bowl. As well as making nice little fish poops, fish excrete ammonia (nitrogen) wastes. Humans also excrete nitrogenous wastes in the form of urea, or urine. There is no mechanical filter that is small enough to sort one molecule from another, so another filtration method is required.

Mother Nature to the rescue! Remember all that stuff I said about natural systems and parts of a pond working together? Here is where it really comes into play. There are naturally occurring bacteria that will eat the dissolved waste products and thus remove them from your pond. This process is called biological filtration. The key to a good biofilter is to provide a lot of surface area the bacteria can attach to and grow.

Important Job
One of the most important jobs at the koi show is the continuous testing of the show tank water to make sure that it is not toxic to fish.

Chemical Filtration

Chemical filtration is the use of a chemical compound to remove certain types of dissolved wastes. This type of filter is not especially common in pond-keeping, but it can serve some very important functions in emergency situations. Zeolite, for example, can remove ammonia fish wastes. This is very handy if you are transporting a koi and it is confined to a very small container; you will also often see little baggies of zeolite in the show tanks at koi shows. In these circumstances there are many large fish in a very small amount of water.

Filter Materials

You will see all sorts of materials used in pond filter boxes, but you really are looking for two qualities when considering filter materials. First, the material absolutely must be non-toxic to fish. Some materials not originally intended for ponds may have been treated with chemicals such as germicides or fire retardants that are toxic to your fish. Second, the material needs to have lots of surface area for the friendly bacteria to grow on. I have very specific advice on filter packing. First, if you buy a commercial filter, you won't have to worry about it; just use the filter material that was included. But if you are a do-it-yourself kind of person like me, choose materials that have these characteristics:

√ Lots of surface area

√ Open space for water flow

√ Fish-grade, non-toxic materials

√ Offers the best value in terms of surface area per dollar

√ Easy to rinse clean.

Also, if you buy a complete filter, the materials may wear out over time and you will need to know where to go for a good replacement. Filter mats will eventually wear out, and you can replace them with new mats or a good high-surface-area packing material.

Having many fish in a pond requires heavy filtration.

Filter Brushes

Filter brushes are a staple of pond-keeping in the United Kingdom and are now starting to make an appearance in the United States. Filter brushes offer some advantages as a prefilter material where you are trying to remove some of the heavier bulk solids before you pass the water through a finer screen.

What is really neat is that you can jostle the brushes and hose them off to remove the debris at cleaning time. They also have lots of surface area for bacterial growth, but their main utility is to remove solids. Filter brushes also make a good breeding material for koi.

Foam and Filter Mats

Filter foam is similar to the foam in your couch, but the pores (the little air pockets) are larger and, hopefully, they are connected. Filter foam has a lot of surface area, which is good.

The drawbacks of foam are that it clogs easily, and as it clogs the interior surfaces get cut off from fresh flowing water, thus reducing its utility as a biofilter. My opinion is that filter foam makes a good top layer or solids removal material–just expect to be cleaning it fairly frequently.

In a filter using filter foam, it is easiest to have two or three pieces of the foam ready to go. You remove the used piece from your filter when it clogs and put in one of the spares. You can then hose off the used piece and keep it ready for the next change.

Filter mats are similar. Instead of foam, they are made of nonwoven fibers jumbled up in a mat. You can buy very open mats with lots of space between the fibers or fine mats with tighter fiber spacing. Filter mats will suffer from the same problem as foam.

I like filter mats a little better than foam. The structure is a little more conducive to water flow. You can use filter mats as prefilters for solid material removal and as biofilter material. In the final stages of a filter system, where there are very few solids, the filter mat makes a nice high surface area material for the biofilter.

Toxic Foam

Be careful with foam that is not specifically made for use with fish. Many upholstery foams are treated with chemicals, such as fire retardants, that could be harmful to your fish.

Bioballs work well in aquaria but are expensive for the average pond.

One drawback is that the material can be difficult to clean. The debris can be blown out of the mat with a garden hose, but it takes some time.

Bioballs

You will commonly find bioballs in filters for saltwater aquaria and will also see little containers of these funky little balls for sale in aquarium shops and catalogs. They are ghastly expensive for use in a fish pond if you buy them this way. The big benefit of bioballs is that they have a nice open structure for lots of water flow and lots of area for biological growth. Find a fish farming supply catalog and buy them that way to save money.

Odds and Ends

Surface area is the name of the game. The more surface area in your filter medium, the more good bacteria will grow to provide biological filtration. You will find a vast array of plastic items that can be used as media for a biological filter. Things that are commercially available include plastic ribbon materials, plastic pot scrubbers (yup, just like in your kitchen), bioball look-alikes, and some materials that are borrowed from other industries to make rigid plastic packing. You will also see folks use various household items for biofilter materials: plastic hair curlers, packing peanuts, scrub pads, pillow stuffing– you name it, I've seen it.

Siporax

Siporax is an extremely porous glass material formed into little short tubes. The manufacturer recommends its use in water that is very clean. If the water has organic materials, the medium can grow bacteria that slime over the pores and make it useless. It is a little expensive but is a really interesting material.

My recommendation is to consider its use if you are keeping your fish indoors for the winter. You will need a very efficient filter to keep them in a smaller container for the winter months, and you will be able to prefilter the water much better in a small tank or aquarium, which will allow the Siporax to work optimally. I have not used this material yet, but it is a great candidate for a small pond or container garden. I have heard glowing reports from the folks who have tried it.

Rocks

I think rocks make lousy filter material. You will see lots of filters using them, however. The main problem with rocks is that they have little surface area (only the outside of the rock). They also pack tight in a filter, causing problems with water flow. You want the water to contact as much of the filter material as possible. Rocks also clog easily, and it is a royal pain to remove and rinse a bunch of rocks. You will also see lava rock used and touted because of its porous nature. Unless the water is really clean, the pores just slime up and clog. Avoid rocks in your filter box.

Pebbles will work in filters and are cheap, but they clog easily.

Rocks have their use, however. You probably have rocks in your pond. They can provide some of the biological action for the pond. The only type of rock filter that I like is called a stream bed filter. It is a pretty cool idea, and frankly, this is how nature does it. You basically build a long stream full of rocks and let the water run over it. It will work perfectly well. The downside is that eventually it will clog up with gunk and have to be dug out and cleaned. It may take years to clog, but when it does, it's not convenient and it's not fun.

A Surface Area Comparison

Square feet of surface area for each cubic foot of material, followed by relative cost of material (10 = highest cost):

Siporax: 4,100 (3)
Foam: 850 (3)
Plastic scrub pads: 370 (2)
Plastic ribbon: 250 (2)
Bioballs #2: 160 (5)

Bioballs #1: 98 (7)
Bioballs #3: 64 (10)
Half-inch rocks: 50 (1)

The Real Price

When comparing filter materials, just ask what the area per cubic foot is and use it to make your own comparison. Don't forget to factor in the cost, too. You may need a little more material, but if it is inexpensive you may save total dollars.

What is this really telling you? A cubic foot is a box that's one foot on each side. So let's start with the filter foam. A one foot square cube of foam has 850 square feet of surface area for the friendly bacteria (please remember foam is not so great because it clogs easily, but let's keep going). You would need 17 times more rock, three times more plastic ribbon, two times more scrub pads, 13 times more of those really expensive bioballs, and 17 times more rocks to get as much surface area. That's a lot of rocks!

Filter Design Basics

OK, so now you know what types of things you can put into your filter, but how should it be put together? Let's look at the different points you need to consider when designing or selecting a filter for your pond.

How Big Should It Be?

Here is another one of those endlessly debatable issues. The answer is that it depends on your fish load, since the filter will primarily be removing dissolved waste products produced by the fish. The general rule of thumb is to have filter packing material that is 10 to 15% of the pond's water volume. For a 100-gallon pond you thus need 10 gallons of filter material. Extra filter material will not hurt your pond one bit and is an easy way to provide for your growing fish or for the new fish you might buy.

Wait, we are not quite done. How much is 10 gallons of filter? A little quick math is needed to convert gallons to cubic feet. Simply take the number of gallons and divide by 7.5. So for the 100-gallon pond you will need 1.3 cubic feet of filter media.

You can always go with a bigger filter. A little extra area will not hurt. However, the same is not true of your fish. I must caution you about overloading your system with too many fish. You may be able to get away with it for awhile, but as the fish grow the system will become overloaded and you could poison your fish with their own wastes.

Do You Want to Trickle?

If you have seen a saltwater aquarium, you are familiar with the box of bioballs underneath with water trickling over them. The balls are happily growing bacteria, because they need some oxygen below, and the trickle effect enables them to get it. The trickle filter is reported to be more efficient in removing wastes. Guess how many trickle filters I have seen offered for sale for garden ponds? None. I don't exactly know why this is, since theoretically it would be an excellent type.

Instead, you will almost always see the pond filter with its media completely immersed in water. The submerged media filter is much easier to plumb into a pond. If you are going to invest in show koi, aeration of the water in the filter box is a very good idea. If you are pumping up to your filter, a trickle type filter is fine. You will just need to make sure that you have a good way to get all of the packing wet. A spray bar or perforated plate above the filter medium will work well.

The wastes you can see are not as dangerous as the invisible chemicals in the water.

Up or Down Flow

Now we are getting deep into filter design. The water can flow up from the bottom of the filter box or down from the top. What you are trying to achieve is a uniform flow pattern through the filter material. You want every surface of the biofilter to get a constant supply of new water for maximum waste conversion.

Upward is the most efficient way to flow the water through the medium. The filter will usually have a stand pipe in the center that carries the water to the next filter box or back to the pond.

The next best flow pattern is horizontal flow. I have seen this flow pattern used in several commercial filters. My gut feeling is that there may be a fair amount of water that by-passes the medium in these filters. Look for a horizontal flow filter that keeps the filter material snug along the sides of the filter box to minimize any by-pass flow.

Finally, there is downward flow, where the water enters the top of the filter box and exits the filter from the bottom. I think this is a good choice for small filters. Many commercial filters will be set up to work with downward flow. However, downward flow is the least efficient flow pattern in terms of getting all the water to flow through the filter medium. It is usually not difficult to convert a downward flow filter to an upward flow. You will usually add a stand pipe to the center of the filter. If you decide to attempt this, take care when you cut the filter box.

Solids Removal Prefilter

First thing, you need to remove the leaves and large particles. This is probably the most important step to your pond enjoyment. There are a few ways to accomplish this. A well-designed solids removal step keeps the maintenance of the rest of the pond down to a minimum. Solid removal methods that work well include:

√ Settling chambers to slow the water down and allow the solids to drop to the bottom.

√ Skimmer and settling boxes, which are similar to a swimming pool skimmer box but bigger. These are good for removing floating leaves and debris.

√ Filter brushes.

A Sump Section

You need this to house your pump. A sump also gives you some spare room to place any chemical filter materials in your system as needed.

Special Mention Filters
Bubble Bead Filters

These have been around for awhile but have recently become very popular with serious pond-keepers. A bubble bead filter is a closed tank that is filled with floating plastic beads. The water is pumped through the bed of beads from the bottom up. You still need to remove large solids such as leaves before the water gets to the bubble bead filter, so a prefilter is still required.

Reports are that these are great filters for removing solids and for biological filtration. To clean the filter you simply open the drain valve and quickly wash out all of the solids. Some bubble beads have aeration or paddles to really loosen the solids during the cleaning cycle. For a large koi pond, I would definitely check these out.

Sand Filter

A sand filter is similar to a swimming pool or spa filter. It has a can full of coarse sand. While the filter has tons of surface area, it is best used in very clean water. They can often become clogged up with particles and can take forever to wash clean. My recommendation is to pass.

Fluidized Bed Filter

Instead of packed sand, these filters use water flow to keep the sand moving in the filter. These are very popular for aquaria right now. I run one on my 200-gallon aquarium and have been very happy with its performance. For a small pond or container, these will probably work like gangbusters. Look in an aquarium supply catalog for a good one. I think the idea has real merit for larger systems as well.

Vortex Filter

A great low-tech solution to solids removal, vortex filters work very well. A round tank with a conical bottom is fed water in the middle of the container. This sets up a swirling action that allows the solids to drop down to the bottom of the filter chamber. There are systems available with four or more vortex chambers to perform the filtration stages. These are very good filters.

I have noticed that most vortex filter systems offered for sale have top-down flow, when clearly an up-flow design would be much better. If you buy one of these, ask to have it piped for upward flow. Also, just a single vortex chamber as a prefilter step is probably sufficient if you want to use a cheaper box for the biological filter stages.

Homemade filters of all types will work in ponds, but they require tinkering.

Build Your Own

You are now officially a pond filtration expert. You can use these ideas to assemble your own pond filter. There

Finding Filter Media

You can purchase loose filter materials by catalog or can look for plastic high-surface-area items that can be substituted. I recommend that you buy filter media intended for this use so that you take no chance with any toxic chemicals that may be hiding in non-standard materials.

is a huge variety of plastic tubs, buckets, and garbage cans that can be used as filter boxes. Common PVC plumbing can be used to connect several tubs to make a whole filtration system.

I have built my own filters and once had a four-stage garbage can filter. It eventually worked very well. "Eventually" means I made some mistakes at first. Here's a list of what I learned from my mistakes, so that you can skip over my long learning curve.

√ Use larger fittings for the best water flow.

√ Use at least 3-inch-diameter fittings and valves for drains.

√ Don't use rock; it will clog, and it is heavy.

√ Carefully balance the height of the filter boxes so that you don't accidentally drain your pond.

Keep That Water Moving: Pumps

We are deep into the most technical part of this book. Choosing a filter and a pump is very important to your long-term enjoyment of the hobby, and a little math is required. If you are a real fish geek like me, this is the fun part. You get to impress your friends with your superior knowledge. Just imagine all the admiration you will receive at the next pond kegger when you dazzle them with your math skills!

For the less mathematically inclined, I will make it really easy. There's no getting around the fact that these are the tools you will need to select the correct hardware. Keeping your pond clean and your fish healthy will be your rewards for the extra time you take to make a few calculations.

A nice waterfall puts little stress on the proper pump.

I will also give you some very easy rules of thumb that you can go by for pump selection. There will be something for everybody in this chapter.

I Want to Pump You Up!

Pumps are used to move things. There are pumps that can pump water very well and pumps that can pump whole tomatoes in a food factory. Pond-keepers want to pump water.

You already know that if you want to keep more than a very small number of fish, you will need to use a filter. The filter won't work unless you move the water through it. That means you also need a pump. Some filter makers may help you with your pump selection by recommending what pump to buy, but some may not. So how do you know what to pick?

Getting Centrifugal

Many types of pumps have been developed, but I'm not going to talk about them here. That's because more than likely you will be buying a centrifugal pump.

The centrifugal pump is a simple device that converts the energy of an electric motor to kinetic energy. In other words, it makes water move. Water enters the center of the pump. The electric motor turns a shaft, which in turn spins the pump's impeller. The impeller slings the water from the center of the pump to the outside casing and out of the pump.

To pick the most efficient pump, you must consider many different factors

There are two types of centrifugal pumps used for ponds. One type has a direct drive. The shaft of the electric motor connects directly to the impeller. There is a mechanical seal that retains the water in the pump volute (just a fancy word for the casing). An advantage of direct drive pumps is that they are a little more efficient. Disadvantages are the possible need to replace the seal and the fact that they heat the water. Also, the motor and pump usually are not waterproof in this type of pump. Direct drive pumps can be made waterproof by placing the motor in a sealed container filled with oil. The direct drive pump will be your best bet when pumping large volumes of water.

The second type of pump you will see has a magnetic drive. The impeller shaft is attached to a magnet. On the motor side there is another magnet that the impeller shaft rests in. The motor spins its magnet and captures the magnetic field of the shaft magnet, making it spin. What is neat is that there is no direct connection of the impeller to the motor. The pump and motor can be totally enclosed and fully submersible. Advantages are that there are no mechanical seals that can leak, less heat is given off, and it is submersible. Disadvantages are less efficient pumping and limited availability for large flows.

Determine Your Flow Rate

There are some rules of thumb you will see for picking pumps. Really, these are rules for figuring out your flow rate. Just going by flow may let you down because you have not accounted for all of your fittings and tubing. But let's start with flow.

When you read other pond books, you will come across what I find to be confusing terminology. You will see the phrases *turnover* and *pond volume*. I think people have mistakenly used these two terms interchangeably, but they are really different. That's why I want to take a stand and be very clear about how I will define these vague terms.

Big Pipes

Remember that small diameter pipes increase head loss, so try to use the largest diameter piping anywhere in the pond that you can get away with it. Large diameter piping also clogs less easily and puts less stress on the pump.

• Pond volume: Easy! This is the volume of water in your pond, period. You will see recommendations like "one pond volume every hour." This means if your pond is 1,000 gallons, your pump should move around 1,000 gallons of water per hour. Got it? How easy can it get?

• Turnover: Now this is a different beast. You need to do a little math to calculate this guy. A turnover is the time OR flow rate required to filter a certain percentage of all of the water in the pond. Keep reading! I promise your head won't explode over this one.

Imagine your pond for a moment. The water flows into your filter and is pumped back into the pond. The water that has just been filtered will mix with the "dirty" water that's in the pond and dilute the dirty water. So how do you really get every bit of the pond water through the filter in your desired "turnover" per hour? Let's skip the mathematical rigmarole and go straight to the solution.

The flow formula: $F = K(V/T)$

The time formula: $T = K(V/F)$, where

K is an efficiency constant

V is the total volume of the pond

T is the time in hours for a complete turnover

F is the flow rate in gallons per hour.

The efficiency constant (K) is based on the percentage of water filtered. For 99% it is 4.6; for 99.9% it is 6.9; and for 99.99% it is 9.2.

Waterfalls need a bit more flow.

You still with me? Great! Just a little more. I think 99% of all the pond water going through the filter is good enough. Remember the 1,000-gallon pond that will be filtered at a flow rate of 1,000 gallons per hour? How many hours will it take for 99% of the pond water to turn over? I need to use the time formula for this one:

Time = K (4.6) x [V (1,000 gallons) / F (1,000 gallons per hour)]

Time = 4.6 x 1 = 4.6 hours

So in 4.6 hours 99 percent of my pond water has gone through the filter. That will give me about five turnovers in a day. Cool!

The Bottom Line on Flow Rate

After all of this, what is the bottom line? The bigger the pond, the fewer times you must turn it over in a day. But it all really depends on the fish load in the system. In an aquarium you would like to turn over 99% of the water in an hour because in an aquarium you have many fish in a small volume. In a pond you will have fewer fish in a larger amount of water.

The surfaces in your pond also offer some biological filtering action. Every rock, pebble, and even the liner will help you some. When you compare the surface area of all this stuff in a pond to the surface area in an aquarium, you can also see why you don't need as much flow through the filter of a pond.

As a general rule, based on 99% turnover, you would want to turn your pond over as follows:

Up to 100 gallons: 1 turnover per hour, 4 to 5 pond volumes per hour

100 to 1,000 gallons: 6 turnovers per day, 1 to 2 volumes per hour

1,000 to 5,000 gallons: 4 turnovers per day, 75% to 1 volume per hour

5,000 gallons and up: 2 to 3 turnovers per day, 40% to 60% volume per hour.

Head Loss

As water goes through the pump, pipe, couplings, valves, and other segments of the plumbing, it faces resistance in the form of friction at the sides of the plumbing. In this way some of the pumping force of the pump is lost, a reaction technically called head loss. In a large pond with many yards of piping and all sorts of plumbing combinations, head loss can be significant and reduce the movement of water through the pond to quite a bit less than the theoretical pumping ability of the pump. The calculations to determine head loss are quite complicated, and for most situations they probably are unnecessary. Pond-keepers tend to compensate for head loss by buying a somewhat

Every surface in the pond aids biological filtration and decreases needed flow.

Not Suitable

Very large ponds will require higher flow rates, which means a bigger pump. It is difficult to find submersibles that are economical at high flow rates. You will be better off with a pump that must be connected to your pond externally.

larger pump than they would need without loss and by using the largest diameter piping and couplings possible. Water flowing through a small diameter pipe loses more force than when it flows through a wider pipe, which of course makes sense. If you really want to determine head loss, consult with a contractor or professional pond builder.

Scotty, I Need More Power!

How much will it cost to power the motor for the pump? You certainly don't want to make all the lights in the neighborhood dim when you start it up, and you also want the most bang for your kilowatt-hour bucks.

Calculating the cost to run your pump is easy. Just look at the amperage rating of the pump, which is provided by the manufacturer. Multiply that by 115 volts (unless you have installed a 220-volt pump) to obtain the total watts of electricity used by the pump each hour. For example, a 2.8-amp pump uses 322 watts an hour (2.8 x 115 = 322). You'll run your pump 24 hours a day, 7 days a week, so in a 30-day month you'll run it 720 hours. Make sense so far?

To figure out how much it will cost to run the pump each month in a 1,000-gallon pond, all you still need to know is the cost of your local electricity. In my area the calculation would look like this:

Cost = (Watts x Hours Operated x Power Cost) / 1,000

Cost = (322 watts x 720 hours x $0.08 per kilowatt-hour) / 1,000

Cost = $18.55 per month. That's $223 per year.

This is a good estimate of the power usage. It is possible that your pump will actually use less power if you are running close to the best efficiency point. This number represents *the most* it should cost to run your new pump.

But wait! If I had only looked a little harder, I could have found a pump that only draws 1.3 amps at the same flow rate. Yup, I'm looking right at one now. Hey, that is going to save me $10 a month–that's $120 a year I can use to buy more koi kibble. It really will be worth your while to look for the pump that uses the least amount of power for your desired flow rate.

Submersible or Not?

You now need to think about the type of pump you want. If you have small flows, it will be best to go with a submersible pump. For a very small pond or container garden, select the correct size powerhead for your flow. Powerheads are little submersible pumps that are used for aquaria. Powerheads are great for small applications.

More fish means bigger filters, means bigger pumps.

Part 2

If you have a bit larger pond, a submersible pump is still very practical and easy to install. Shop around and look for the best flow-per-power-usage you can find. Several of the more popular submersible pumps for ponds are the oil-filled types. I have no particular problem with these and have used them reliably in the past. Some folks report the oil leaks into their pond. This is just a mess. Of course, to completely avoid the *possibility* of oil leaks, look for a magnetically coupled, submersible pump.

Pump Pitfalls

Here is a short trouble-shooting guide that outlines the places where people make mistakes in selecting pumps. Read through this whole section before you purchase your pump. It could save you some bucks.

The Right Pump

Home improvement stores carry all sorts of pumps for different jobs around the house. Most of them are

One Pump, One Job
Pumps are designed for a specific job, and when you ask them to do something different, you will probably not be happy with the result.

Back-siphoning

Remember to prevent back-siphoning. If you have the outlet pipe from your pump submersed in water and the pump turns off and there is a break in the plumbing, the water will suck back through the outlet line and out of your pond. Depending on how you have your water return line placed, you may be looking at the empty pond scenario again. My preference is to place at least one leg of the outlet line open to the air (you can split part to a waterfall and part into the pond). The air will break the siphon.

completely unsuitable as pond pumps. You need to really look into these pumps before you buy. Many of the larger pumps you will find are designed for use as a sump pump or for a sprinkler system. These pumps are designed for periodic use, not constant duty. The mechanical parts of the pump (impeller, seals, and motor) are just not designed for constant use. It is pretty likely that the lifetime of such a pump under constant use will be short, and you will probably be buying a new pump in under a year. Also, because the pump is not designed for constant use, it probably sucks up electricity like a sponge. You will have a huge electricity bill. I don't want you to get turned off to pond-keeping because your pump put you in the poor house.

Priming

When you buy your centrifugal pump, pay careful attention to whether it is called self-priming or not. Many centrifugal pumps require you to prime the pump before you operate it. What that means is that the volute (casing) of the pump must be full of water (in pump lingo that is called flooded) before you start it. Otherwise the air gets trapped in the volute and the impeller wastes energy spinning around with lots of air and little water.

So how do you prime a pump? First, the piping to the inlet of the pump must be as large as the inlet fitting on the pump itself. It's even better if it is larger. Second, you can either pour water into the volute at the pump outlet to fill it up or bleed the outlet to get the pump started. When you start up the pump, you let it pump until you see a lot of water coming out. When you first bleed the pump you may see air and water spraying out until all of the air is expelled,

Dry Danger

Don't operate a pump dry. You will damage the pump because it will heat up and the seals can fail. Let me give you a trick for preventing this from happening. First, imagine you had some sort of break in your plumbing while you were away. Your pump would just keep humming along, emptying the pond. You would come home to an empty pond, dead fish, and a fried pump. Bad. The fix is easy. Install a level control on the pump. You can pick up a simple level control at your home improvement store. The level control floats in the pond, and you set it so that if the water drops below a certain level, the level control shuts off the pump.

Clear water lets you really enjoy your fish.

Part 2

Call the Plumber!

Now that you know all about filters and pumps, you can put the final touches on your filter system. You will need to provide some plumbing to your pond to connect the pump and filter. You will also want to install the plumbing in a way that makes your pond easy to maintain. It is really a pain in the drain to have to redo the plumbing. Planning ahead, especially with plumbing, is a must for large projects and for smaller ponds, too.

Piping

There are many types of tubes and piping that are convenient and easy for the pond hobbyist. Let's take a look at them and where they can be best used. Here are some rules of thumb to go by when selecting pipe or tubing:

Not everyone is able to do their own plumbing, but it can be a fun hobby.

√ Do not use piping that is smaller than the diameter of the pump discharge.

√ Don't use very long stretches of pipe with pumps with low pumping power.

√ Choose pipe that is sturdy and easy to work with.

√ Select pipe that is safe to use for drinking water.

Part 2

Freezing PVC

PVC pipe and fittings become brittle at temperatures below freezing. Place PVC items in a protected place so that you don't accidentally run over them with the riding mower or bump them hard in the winter, or you may find yourself fixing broken pipes.

Getting used to working with piping is essential for the pond enthusiast.

All About Pipe

Pipe has standard diameters that are agreed on by the industry. There are standards so that users are assured that the sizes are consistent. Standards and specification also form a framework for manufacturers to produce high-quality products. Finally, by using standardized products, end users can design piping systems that work properly and safely. Just imagine if every company made pipe with slightly different dimensions. How could you ever make fittings for every possible diameter?

The dimensions that you see in the store are called the nominal dimensions. One-inch "nominal" diameter PVC pipe has an outside diameter of 1.313 inches. You will also see the word "schedule" to describe pipe. The schedule tells you the thickness of the walls of the pipe. These dimensions are also agreed upon standards. A "one"-inch diameter pipe will have different inside diameters depending on the "schedule" number. The higher the schedule number, the thicker the walls of the pipe. For example, schedule 40 pipe has an inside diameter of 1.049 inches, while schedule 80 pipe has an inside diameter of 0.957 inches.

You can see that the term "one-inch pipe" has a lot more to do with the inside diameter of the pipe. That really makes sense since that is where the water flows. It also makes lots of sense that the outside diameter is always the same. This way the connectors can be made by different companies and fit all the pipes out there.

Water systems can have different working pressures. A thicker walled pipe is designed for safe use in higher pressures. Burst pipes can do plenty of damage. So why not just have a standard thickness? The answer is cost. Thicker pipe costs more. (You will notice this when you shop for pipe.) With different thicknesses you can choose the pipe that is safe and most economical for your use.

Why Not Metal?

Pipes are made in many materials, and in your local store you will probably see several types. My advice is to ignore any metallic material unless you have some special reason to use it. Metal pipe is hard to work with. It is hard to cut, hard to put threads on, and relatively expensive. Use plastic everywhere you can. PVC is inexpensive, easy to use, and available everywhere.

The Truth About Tubing

Tubing is also very handy for water garden projects. Tubing is easy to identify in the stores since it usually comes on rolls. There are different materials and sizes commonly available. Here is what you need to look for:

√ Buy tubing that is OK for drinking water so it will be safe for use with fish.

√ Don't buy tubing with a very thin wall; it will easily crimp and stop water flow.

√ Use a large enough diameter; too small slows flow and puts stress on the pump.

√ Make sure that you can find fittings.

√ Use hose clamps; leaks are a pain.

Polyethylene tubing is common in home improvement outlets. It is fairly rigid as tubing goes and comes in large rolls. The only hassle about working with it is that you must use the correct fittings to make elbows and bends. If you try to make the tubing turn the corner you may find it kinked later.

Connectors

You can also find a wide variety of connectors and fittings that can help you hook up your tubing to the pump and filter. Just remember that connectors all cause the system to lose pressure. Use as few as possible and keep the runs of tubing as short as possible.

Tubes for Small Projects

For container gardens or small ponds you will probably be using a small submersible pump such as a powerhead. In most cases, flexible tubing will be your best choice. You can purchase clear tubing from your local aquarium retailer or home improvement store. Just make sure it is safe for drinking water.

Beware of tubing that has very thin walls. Thin tubing can collapse and choke the flow of water if the walls are not thick enough.

In a small pond or a container garden, it is best to keep as much of the tubing as possible in the water. This keeps it out of view and makes the whole project look more finished. The filter and other mechanical doodads that keep your fish healthy should also be as invisible as possible. This way, nothing distracts from your lovely little pond.

Here are some ways to hide your filter:

√ Dig a hole or sump beside your pond where you keep the filter. Make sure that you do not drop it below the level of the pond, or it will overflow.

√ Use a large plastic tub as a sump.

√ Use a plastic tub that will cover your pond filter. Hide the tub with plants, rocks, or whatever will look nice.

√ Many pond and garden stores sell a false hollow rock that can cover a filter. Use some real rocks around it to keep it from looking too fake.

Piping for Midsize Projects

As your project gets larger, the piping becomes a bigger deal. With small projects you can fuss around with tubing and little connectors until you get it just right. As things get bigger, more care will be needed to make sure you get it right the first time. It's easy to snip off little bits of plastic tubing and snug them over powerhead outlets. Laying and relaying pipe is another story.

Big Enough

If you are using a submersible pump, select pipe or tubing that is at least as large as the pump discharge. If it is too small you will have too much pressure loss and your filter may not get the flow rate you expected.

Large Ponds

You will not have many options when you build a large pond. Your best choice for plumbing is PVC. It is available in large diameters, like 3 and 4 inches. You will also find that valves and fittings are more expensive as you get to the larger diameters. Don't let that fact stop you from making the investment. Using piping that is too small for the application is one of the biggest mistakes you can make. If the piping is too small you will not get enough flow and will have too much pressure loss. If the drain pipe is too small you won't get enough flow to really sweep the solids out the drain, and you will wait forever for your drain. Drains should whoosh, not dribble.

Drains

I can't think of anything that can make pond-keeping easier than the correct drains. Always make a drain a large as practical. Waiting for water to drain is boring. A large drain also allows the water to flow from the filter box with some velocity, which is great for carrying mulm away.

You will want to occasionally wash solids, gook, and mulm out of the filter. The drain lets you open a valve to drain it out, and you can use your garden hose to wash things into the filter.

You need somewhere for the water from all drains to go. Most pond-keepers position the drains so that they are downhill from the pond and somewhat out of sight. It depends on your preference, but I used to just run the drain water out into my woods. If your filter is in a sump, run the drains out of the sump and away from the pond.

Drains for filter boxes can be assembled with a few simple fittings. First you need a proper bulkhead fitting. A short length of pipe or tubing, followed by a valve, completes your simple drain.

Big Drains

Always install a larger drain than you think you need. There is nothing more frustrating than waiting around for something to drain. In large ponds, go for a drain that is at least 2 inches in diameter.

A large, properly installed drain will make any pond easier to maintain.

Large or small, simple or complex, your pond needs a drain.

Bottom Drains

Don't forget to install a drain in the bottom of your pond. It is a good idea to completely drain and muck out your water garden once in a while. I usually do this once in the fall and sometimes in the spring, depending on how gooey it looks on the bottom of the pond.

Large ponds should have special bottom drains installed. My advice is to purchase bottom drains specifically designed for ponds. These drains can be used to collect detritus from the bottom of the pond. I think opening the bottom drain once a week to remove mulm is probably sufficient. (Of course, you don't let all the water drain out; just the little bit of nasty brown stuff on the bottom.) However, if you have a high fish load or are keeping very fancy koi, continuously removing mulm is a good idea. Just attach the bottom drain to the filter for continuous removal.

Special bottom drains are a little harder to find. You will probably have to purchase one from a special dealer or a specialty catalog for fish or koi ponds.

Skimmers

You have probably seen a swimming pool skimmer. It has an overflow box and draws in water from the surface of the pool, filters out any large bits of detritus, then returns the water to the pool. These are handy, especially if you have many leaves that drop into the pond. A pool skimmer can be incorporated into your pond design, or you can purchase one that is specifically designed for ponds. A simple standpipe can also be used as a skimmer and is very easy to make on your own.

Skimmers can cause a few minor problems. Most fish food floats, so your skimmer could remove most of it before the fish get a chance to eat. Small fish and tadpoles could also take a ride in the skimmer. I think it is best to design the skimmer so that the runoff goes to a separate box where you can easily remove the skimmer debris and retrieve any hapless critters that went into the skimmer.

Hiding Filters

Often filters are placed in the ground to hide them. Because of gravity, the water in your filter will want to be level with the water in the pond. If you put the filter below the level of the pond, your filter will overflow! The filter water level must be even with the pond water level.

Ponds and streams will overflow at times, so be prepared.

Pond Overflow

There are times when your pond may have too much water in it. You will certainly experience a heavy rainfall. The snow and ice will melt in the spring. If you are a klutz like me, you might decide to add a little water to your pond and leave the hose on all day!

A simple standpipe in your pond can work for you as an overflow. Don't forget to place some type of screen or grate over the top of the pipe to prevent any of your fish from washing away.

You could also build a dry stream bed that runs away from your pond. For a dry stream to work well, you should place it on the down-hill side of the pond. You can add plantings to make it look pretty, but remember that water will flow in your stream occasionally.

Other Handy Fittings

Quick disconnects come in a variety of sizes that can make pond clean-up chores a breeze. They enable you to quickly attach hoses to drains. Gate valves are harder to find and more expensive, but these are the best valves to use for ponds. Ball valves are common and are easy to use, but they can be a problem in cold climates, where they can freeze up and break. I usually go with them anyway, unless there is an obvious need for

Part 2

Part 2

You Be the Plumber

The best way to think of plumbing is that it is an adult tinker toy set. You will be amazed at the wide variety of different types of pipe, tubing, and all those different connectors! If you are plumbing phobic, building your own water garden is an excellent remedy. Tackle your plumbing project confidently. The worst thing you can do is get wet, and that really isn't so bad!

a gate valve. Check valves are one-way valves that prevent your system from backing up if the pump power is interrupted.

Shopping

I have found that there are several locations to look in a store to find the fittings, tubing, and piping that you need for your project. The most obvious place to look is in the plumbing section. You will find PVC piping and fittings in many sizes here. You will also find the other accessories that you will need to work with PVC in the plumbing section.

Tubing is trickier. I have found the fittings and tubing in a variety of sections. It may be in the plumbing section, which makes life much easier. Don't stop there, however. Look for parts for do-it-yourself underground sprinkler systems. (That's where I usually find hose barbs for tubing.) Also, don't forget the garden section. You might find various fittings hiding out there.

Hiding the filter takes some thought and effort.

I have spent hours wandering around stores looking for hose barbs to fit some particular tubing that I am using. It usually is worth the effort. When I cannot find what I need locally, I go to catalogs or the Internet. The really unusual or hard to find items are usually in these more complete sources.

Working With Plumbing

I have found that a few tools are very useful for working with plumbing. A rubber mallet is great for tapping fittings firmly into place. A small hand saw is needed for cutting PVC pipe and some tubing. A sharp knife or scissors can be used to cut softer tubing. Don't forget hose clamps if you are working with tubing. You can find these at automotive supply stores, too.

For small projects, use tubing; it is much easier to work with. For larger projects, I recommend PVC pipe and fittings. You can find both threaded and slip fittings for PVC. The slip fittings are easiest to work with. A slip fitting slides onto the pipe and is bonded with PVC glue. I have found that for many projects I don't need to use the PVC glue. I tap the fittings firmly into place with a rubber mallet and get a good seal. This lets me easily change things later. If the fittings were glued, you would have to saw them off to make any changes. However, on a large project plan on using the glue when you have everything plumbed where you need it.

Be careful not to gouge or scratch the inside of a PVC slip fitting. The scratch can create a leak. You would have to replace the fitting to fix it.

An easy way to work with PVC is to build the plumbing as you go, just like tinker toys. You place your fitting on the filter, place the pipe, and then cut it off where you want it. Next you put on a fitting and keep going. It really is easy. The nice thing about PVC plumbing is that it is pretty cheap and you can just start again if you make a mistake.

Hose Barbs

A hose barb is a plumbing connector that has at least one connector that is specifically made for a tube or hose. It is called a barb because the end is tapered with ridges to help hold the hose in place. Don't forget to also use a hose clamp! Even with a tight fit on a barb, the hose can still come off.

Part 2

Winning the Plumbing Game

There are two goals to collecting all of those plumbing parts. The first goal is to make your life easier. You want to make it as easy as possible to do the routine chores of keeping your pond. The easier and faster they are to complete, the more time you will have to enjoy your water garden. You need to have drains that will remove water and waste quickly. You need to have a filter that is easy to clean. You need to have the water circulating in your pond in a way that brings oxygen to your fish and moves waste to the filter. Here are some hints that will make things easier for you:

PVC pipes and fittings allow you to create many pond effects.

√ Buy valves that are easy to open and close. PVC ball valves do not work well in the cold. Consider gate valves in cold climates.

√ Drains should be placed in the filter, the bottom of the pond, and within streams and waterfalls.

√ The drain piping should be large enough to have a fast flow rate. You want to "whoosh" the gunk away.

√ Place your water garden in a place where you can position drains where the water will run away from the pond.

√ Plan a place for your pond water to drain. Can you use it to water another garden? Is there a ditch or drain in your yard that you can use? Do you have some woods to drain it off to? You can use "French drain" piping buried in the ground to get your pond runoff where you want it.

√ Use your garden hose and spray nozzle to wash things out while the drains are open. This works great for filters and waterfalls. Open the valve, let the hose rip, rinse the gunk out.

The second goal you should embrace is to keep the plumbing, filter, and pump as inconspicuous as possible. I have seen ponds large and small where the builder was obviously very proud of their skills with plumbing. There were pipes and valves running every which way about 4 feet into the air behind the pond. You couldn't look at anything else. It was like Frankenstein's lab.

I am sure that the creator was very proud of the accomplishment, but you can be just as proud but much more clever by concealing the plumbing. You want your visitors to ooh and ahh over the fish and magnificent plants, not the plumbing. PVC plumbing is bright white and very obvious, but there are plenty of things you can do to make it less conspicuous. Use your imagination. Here are a few of my ideas:

Fountain, fish, fake heron–but where is the filter hidden?

√ Place plumbing at the back of the pond or container.

√ Put as much plumbing in one place as possible.

√ When you can, bury it in the ground.

√ If it is above ground, conceal it with plants and bushes.

√ When outside of the pond, spray paint white PVC a less obvious color like dark green or brown.

√ Cover external plumbing with landscaping gravel or wood chips.

√ Place rocks, plants, or other objects in front of in the pond plumbing. Don't block the filter inlet or skimmer, though.

Just remember that you want your water garden to look like it has always been there. It should blend in and enhance the landscape, not scare the neighbors.

Putting It All Together

There are many ways that you can connect your filter and pump to your pond. This can get tricky, because you need to think about the possible ways things might go wrong.

If you pump water to the filter, what happens if the filter gets clogged? The pump will keep pumping. It might overflow the water out of the filter and right on out of your pond.

If you have placed the pump after the filter, what happens if the filter is clogged? The pump will not get enough water and will be left running dry. You can ruin your pump forever by running it dry.

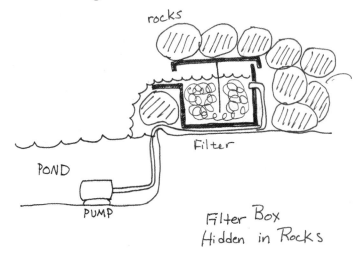

rocks

Filter

POND

PUMP

Filter Box
Hidden in Rocks

Filters should work but not be
seen. Keep them hidden.

Part 2

Stop & Go

Starting and stopping is not so great for the pump. Each time it starts, it uses more electricity than when it is in running mode.

So what is a new pond-builder to do? There are a few setups that will work fine for you. The way you set up the filter and pump will also depend on how big are the filter and pump. Let's start with smaller filters.

Filters

You can set up the filter to be part of your waterfall. You will have the pump send the water up to the filter, where the filter outlet goes right back to the pond. In most cases you will find it easiest to select a submersible pump. How do you avoid problems with this setup?

The filter needs some way for the water to by-pass the filter material and go back to the pond. Many commercially available filters have been designed this way. Often the filter medium is just by-passed. The type of filter that may give you problems here is one where the water comes into the top of the filter and there is a filter pad right on top. If that pad clogs, the water can flow out the top of the filter box. One way to fix this is to cut the top pad so that it does not cover the entire surface of the filter box. Then, as the pad clogs, the water will spread out across the pad; when the whole pad is clogged, the water just by-passes the pad.

Visitors want to look at your pond, not your plumbing.

You can also use a filter that is submerged in the pond. If it gets clogged up, the pump is also submerged and begins to pump less water, but since it is submerged in water, it just spins uselessly. The pump should not be left in that state for too long, because it is generating heat. You will know by the flow coming out of the pump that the filter is clogged.

For larger ponds, the filter and pump will be larger, and you may not be able to use a submersible pump. Here is how I would hook these up. I would build a sump to contain the filter boxes and the pump. The sump must be well-designed so that it is concealed but accessible for cleaning, and it should have its own drain so that it does not fill up with water. The sump should be designed to keep rain water from getting into it. Where there are ponds, there's water, so put a drain on the sump. You never know. I would place the filter boxes so that they were filled by gravity from the pond.

The pump is at the end of the filter boxes. If you are using a submersible pump, I like to have one last filter box that is just for the pump. What if the filter clogs? I like to put a level control on the filter box that the pump is sitting in. If the filter is clogged, the last box will fill slowly or not at all. The pump will shut off before the last box runs out of water. You could end up with a situation where the pump goes on and off, your cue to clean the filter.

You can also use the same setup and install a pump external to the filter boxes. Remember to have the pump close to the bottom of the box and to have a large enough pipe from the box to the pump. You can use the same level control idea here. The level control is in the last filter box. It shuts off the pump if the water level drops.

Other Equipment to Consider

I have covered the major equipment that you will need for keeping more than just a few fish in your pond–the filter and pump. But what would a complete ensemble be without accessories? Let's talk about some of the accessory items you can install that will increase your enjoyment of the hobby.

Adding Air

Fish breathe the same way we do. They need oxygen and have a special organ–the gills–to remove it from the water. If there is not enough dissolved oxygen in the water they drown. Holy cow! Did you ever think a fish could drown?

There are times where the oxygen level in your pond can become low, very low. For example, the hotter the water gets, the less oxygen it holds. Hot summers can be very stressful on your fish, especially if they are starving for oxygen.

The bacteria that make your filter do its job also require oxygen. Without oxygen, the deep areas of your pond and filter can go anaerobic. That's just a fancy way to say they are without oxygen. In such circumstances the good bacteria that help to break down wastes die. The bad bacteria that thrive without oxygen begin to convert the solid wastes in the pond

> ## DO
> *Dissolved oxygen* (usually abbreviated as DO) is an odd concept, but all sorts of things dissolve in each other. When you add salt to water, the salt molecules mix up with the water molecules. The salt seems to go away, but one taste lets you know that it is still there. The same thing happens with oxygen in water.

A useful waterfall doesn't have to be fancy.

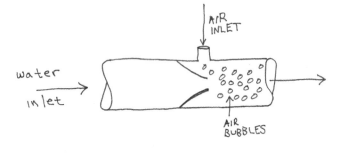

Venturi
cut away view

A venturi adds air to the moving water.

into some really nasty things, such as hydrogen sulfide gas. Hydrogen sulfide stinks like rotten eggs, is very toxic, and can kill all of your fish.

Waterfalls and Fountains

I think you should get the biggest bang for your pumping dollars. By using the filter's pump to add air to your system, you make it do double duty. A waterfall or fountain is an easy way to mix air into the water, and it also looks great. You can also use a spray nozzle to jet fine streams of water back into the pond. As the water flies through the air, it will pick up oxygen and bring it back into the pond. Just don't send all of your pump outlet through the nozzle. You may reduce your flow rate too much and cause your filter to fail. A simple T-fitting in the exit line of your filter can be used to divert part of the flow back to the spray nozzle.

The Venturi

The venturi is a cool little gizmo that uses the change in pressure across a change in pipe diameter to suck air into the water. It looks like a little nozzle or jet inside another pipe. Just before this nozzle is an opening that runs above the water level. Inside the venturi there is a sudden restriction of the water flow. As the water rushes through the nozzle, a vacuum is created behind it; it sucks air into the pipe and mixes it into the water. You can feel the suction if you put your finger over the air flow.

A venturi does not work especially well if the outlet tube is placed far below the surface of the pond, but at shallow depths it's just fine. A venturi will cost you some loss of pumping pressure, but it is well worth planning for in your plumbing design. It is best to make the venturi the very last fitting in the pipe before it goes back into your pond.

Part 2

Airstones

You can maximize the pump's utility by buying a good airstone to place at the end of the air outlet tubing. Airstones are small pieces of porous stone, glass, or wood that will break up the air into tiny bubbles. The smaller the bubbles, the more oxygen that can dissolve in the water.

You don't need extra aeration in a pond, but it's nice to plan for emergencies

Air Pumps

I prefer the "free" methods of getting oxygen into your pond, such as waterfalls and sprays, but having an air pump around for emergencies is a very good idea. An aquarium air pump is sufficient for small to midsize ponds.

These are simple diaphragm pumps. In a diaphragm pump, a piece of rubber or a little rubber cup (the diaphragm) is moved up and down. When the diaphragm is pulled down, air is sucked in one side. When the diaphragm is pushed up, the air is pushed out the other side. Small one-way valves built into the air pump keep the air moving in the right direction.

If you have a large pond, and especially if you are a koi-keeper, using an airstone in the biological filter is usually recommended. The filter will work much more efficiently if it gets plenty of oxygen.

Air Emergencies

There are times where you may need a way to get some air to your pond. If the weather is very warm, your fish may start to gasp at the surface, looking for more oxygen. You may also have a few sick fish that are under medication. The extra oxygen can really

Airstone Materials

Wooden airstones deliver a very nice stream of fine bubbles. Watch out though, because they eventually rot away. They are inexpensive, so keep a few spares around. Ceramic airstones can wear out, too, but generally have a longer life.

help them. Additional aeration can also help your fish if there is a large algal bloom in the pond, especially at night. An aquarium-size air pump with airstones should be on hand to give your fish a helping hand.

If you have a power outage that lasts longer than several hours, your filter may go anaerobic, which means all your good bacteria will die. You don't want that. There are battery-powered air pumps available for aquarium use. It is best to be prepared for an emergency.

The UV Clarifier

UV means ultraviolet light. Light comes in many wavelengths, some of which we can see and some of which we can't. Ultraviolet light is a high-energy light that is beyond the visible spectrum. It can be used very effectively to kill cells. It can also give you a sunburn.

You may not yet have seen the lovely pea green water that is common to garden ponds. This is caused by a single-celled alga that loves sun, fertilizer (fish poop), and water—all the things your pond provides. It is ugly and keeps you from getting a good look at your fish.

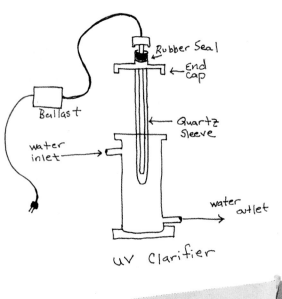

General plan for a UV clarifier.

UV Caution

Please don't look at that light! It will damage your eyes. Make sure the light is off before you do any work on the unit. As with all things electrical around the pond, be sure to buy a UV clarifier that is designed for outdoor use.

The UV clarifier is a great device for killing such algae and keeping the pond water clear. It works by exposing a flow of water to UV light, which kills the algae. Some folks call these devices sterilizers, but the pond water is not really sterile when using the UV clarifier. Of course, you could really zap the water and make it truly sterile, but that truly is overkill when all you want to do is get rid of that green water.

Ultraviolet light does not travel through normal glass very well, so a special quartz glass is used to separate the UV bulb from the water. Clarifiers are simple flow-through devices that can be easily plumbed into the filter system, so the water will be exposed to the UV light as it flows through your filter. Small ponds can use small clarifiers up to 30 watts, and larger ponds will usually be fine with a 60-watt unit.

> ### You Light Up My Life
>
> There are very nice low-wattage garden lights that can be used in the landscaping around your pond. You could also install lights right in the pond. These have been used in swimming pools for a long time, and the new models are very nice and very safe. You only need one to make a nice splash of light in the pond. Some even come with colored lenses. Don't forget your ground fault interruption circuit for any electrical device in the pond.

Ultraviolet bulbs degrade over time. Even though you can see the evil blue glow, the killing wavelength of light is greatly degraded. You should replace your bulb each pond season.

Clean It Up

Last but not least, you will need a few things around to keep your pond looking neat. Here is a shopping list to make clean-up easier.

√ Skimmer net–just like the ones you see for swimming pools. This is very handy for removing fallen leaves and other debris that may fall in.

√ Buckets. I think you should have at least one very large bucket in case you need a place to temporarily keep a fish or water plants. Smaller buckets are great for mixing pond chemicals.

√ Hose. You need to add water somehow.

√ Fish nets. Plan to have a couple of fish nets around in case you need to capture a fish or animal that is in your pond.

√ Flow meter. If you can find a little flow meter with a totalizer, you can easily measure the volume of your pond as you fill it. A totalizer is just like a gas pump. It measures how much water has gone by and keeps adding up the gallons as it goes.

√ Measuring cups. Have a few that are just for adding chemicals to your pond.

√ Scrub brush. Get one with soft bristles; it's good for loosening algae from whatever. Be careful about using hard-bristle brushes on your liner.

Part Three
Construction Zone

"The Smith family, hound, and Olympic-sized garden pond."

Location, Location, Location

Let's leave the technical part of starting your garden pond behind and get on to the more creative work of picking a spot. As you gaze out over your yard, trying to decide the best place for your pond, you will need to keep your equipment in mind—because you are going to do everything possible to hide it! Who wants to look at that pump chugging away? Pond geeks like me do, but you don't want to scare your fish with all that technology out where they can see it. Goldfish are simpletons, and that stuff scares them...really.

Start looking around your yard and your existing garden. Where would a pond look the best? What about the trees you already have? How big will the pond be? What shape? There is a lot to think about.

Get the lay of the land before you start your pond.

Factors to Consider

A Room With a View

I think a lot of people don't consider putting their pond as close to the house as possible, and they should. Some of the loveliest ponds I have seen can be nicely viewed from a room inside the house.

There are plenty of advantages to placing your pond close to the house. You essentially double your enjoyment by being able to peek out and see what is going on out there, even when you're inside. You can enjoy the fish and flowers while watching the football game. You can even feed the fish in your underwear without causing too much alarm among the neighbors.

If you cannot put it very close, do consider putting the pond in view of a door or window as a safety measure. That way you can quickly take a look to make sure nobody fell in or to see if the neighborhood raccoon has come by for a snack.

Let There Be Light

Water plants require a lot of light. Lilies and lotus plants, especially, need plenty of light to thrive and bloom. Algae are also plants, but you will not want to grow them in abundance in your pond. I will talk about ways to combat them later, but starving your pond of light is not one of the ways. It will be easier to deal with too much light than too little.

The amount of shade your pond should receive will be a function of your geographic location and the length of the growing season. The farther north you are, the longer you will want your pond to have full sun. Plan for at least five hours of full sun in northern climates. In the South, plan for shade in the afternoon if possible. Southern ponds can become very hot in the summer months if placed where they receive full sun all day. You will still need at least three hours of full sun for lilies.

No shade at all? Then this is a good time to think about where you could plant some nice trees to shade the pond. Evergreens have the added bonus of not loosing their leaves in the winter months and polluting your pond with them. But what if your yard is too shady? You may have to shop a little harder for your plants, but there are some plants that do not require a lot of sunlight. We'll talk about plantings a bit later..

Take a Load Off

The final thing to think about when you are placing your pond is your comfort. You will want to sit nearby. A patio, deck, or other area for sitting will be very nice. Pondside is also a great place to have your summer parties. Your guests will be envious of all your hard work.

If you already have a deck and are thinking of putting the pond next to it, find out if the deck is made of pressure-treated lumber. Many are. The lumber is treated with arsenic compounds to prevent the wood from rotting. The problem is that runoff from the deck into your pond could hurt your fish. You must prevent rain water from washing over pressure treated lumber and into your pond.

Tree Problems

Trees add complications other than shade. They have large roots that you will damage by digging under. (Or the large roots will damage you when you try to dig under them.) Worst of all, they drop all kinds of junk into your pond that you will just have to fish out later. You will probably find that a good place for your pond is far enough away from the trees so they don't cause a problem.

Flag It

Here is a weekend project that will help you decide the best place to put your pond. Get some of those little plastic flags on sticks that are used by surveyors. You can pick them up at any home improvement store. Now spend the day following the shade around your yard. Write the time on the flag and then stick it in the ground at the edge of the shadow. This way you will know exactly how much of the pond will be shaded each hour. You will probably be surprised to find that shade doesn't only exist right under your trees. You need to search for the right distance from the trees to balance the shade and sun.

The Lay of the Land

Now you need to get a feeling for the contours and elevations of your yard. Hills can enhance the interest of your pond—imagine it nestled into a valley with a hill rising gently behind. Of course, setting your pond into a hill will require you to do more digging. It always amazes me that even a small hill ends up being a bigger dig than you first expected.

There's an even more obvious fact to consider: Water runs downhill. Not too profound, but you will see how this becomes important when you start installing your pond. You see,

A pond in a low spot soon turns into a stagnant hole.

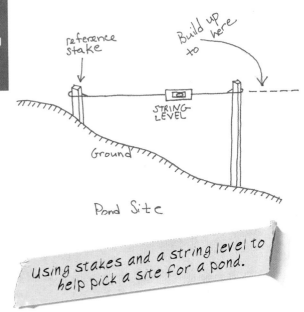

reference stake

Build up here to

STRING LEVEL

Ground

Pond Site

Using stakes and a string level to help pick a site for a pond.

you will need to level your building site, or else the water will not be level in your pond. If you are building on a slope, a terraced effect will work very nicely, but this requires moving a lot of dirt. As you dig dirt out of the higher side of the hill, you will probably need to use it to build up the low side to make your terrace.

Here are some other things to keep in mind when you're looking at your elevations:

√ A pond in the lowest place in the yard will fill up with rain water and runoff to make a swampy spot worse.

√ A pond placed on the highest spot will look strange–like a volcano.

√ If you want a waterfall or stream, remember that water runs downhill. Gravity is your friend.

Level Headed

Water will always be level. If your pond is lower on one side than the other, the water will look shallow on one end and slop over the other side. Producing a level surface is not hard. There are plenty of gadgets you can buy at your local hardware store to help you out–everything from a simple string level to a laser level. I like string levels because they are so easy to use.

A string level is a little tube with water and an air bubble inside. When the tube is level, the bubble rests between two marked lines on the tube. To use it, you attach the tube to a piece of string.

The first step is to get a bunch of stakes and place them in the ground around the area where you will be putting in your pond. Pick one stake to be your reference stake. You will have better luck if you pick a reference stake that is on the uphill side of your project.

Now take a piece of string that is long enough to go from your reference stake to all of the other stakes. Attach your string level near the middle of the string. Oh, by the way, this is much more fun with a buddy. One of you can hold the string, and one of you can tell you when you are level.

Mark a line on the reference stake where you think the top level of your pond will be. Tie the string to the reference stake at that point. Then, take the string to the stake across from it and pull it tight. Now raise or lower the string until your buddy tells you that your string is level. Mark the point on the stake. Repeat the process with all of the stakes, using the same reference stake.

When you're done, you'll know how close to level your site is. You will also know how far up each stake you'll have to build in order to make a level surface as big as your pond. You may find that you need to bring the level up on one or more sides. It may seem easier to just dig the low side further down into the dirt. I don't like doing this, however, because you leave a very low point for rain water and mud to enter the pond. In the long run, it is easier to add soil to the low sides than it is to dig down the high side.

Hidden Treasures

There are many things to consider when you pick a location for your new water garden. You will probably think of all sorts of things you want to be able to see. Did you ever think about the things you don't want to see?

Hiding the Filter

You will probably have some sort of a filter system for even a small pond. Container gardens can even

Rockwork and plants can help hide the filter.

benefit from a small aquarium filter. No matter what size filter, you probably don't want it to be a highlight of your water garden. There are many ways to hide the filter and pump. Here are a few ideas:

√ In small gardens, a submerged pump or filter can be hidden under a small plastic basket (the type designed for planting water lilies). You can put a planted basket on top to conceal it.

√ Build a stand or plateau for your container garden. You can tuck the pump or filter underneath.

√ For larger water gardens, design a sump or sunken chamber that will hold your filter system. Your sump can be covered with a wooden deck that will look very nice with potted plants sitting on top. Make sure to leave some way to get into your sump.

√ Place your water garden on the edge of your yard. You can plant a hedge at the back edge of the pond and place the filter and other equipment out of sight behind the hedge.

√ Hide it in a waterfall. You can build a structure above ground that can contain your filter system. After you have built a strong structure around the filter system, you can use rocks, chickenwire, and mortar to turn it into a waterfall.

Bury a Hose

For convenience, you can bury a strong garden hose protected by PVC pipe. Then at the pond side you can build a little water outlet using a sill cock. (That is the name for hose water spigots that are on the outside of your house.) For a water line, be sure to bury it deeper than the freezing depth of your soil in the winter time.

Hide the Hookups

Your new water garden will require electricity and water. I am sure you will make your water garden safe, but you probably don't want to see an ugly orange electrical cord running across the lawn.

The easiest way to bring the utilities to your new garden and keep them neatly hidden is to bury them. You can make this an easy do-it-yourself project. Your local home improvement store will have plastic pipe that you can use as electrical conduit. It is made of PVC (polyvinyl chloride) and usually is gray. To install an electrical line, it is very easy to use an outdoor outlet. You run an extension cord that is rated for outdoor use inside the conduit, and then bury it. You then just plug it into your

Part 3

outdoor outlet. If your outdoor outlet does not already have a ground fault interrupt circuit, you can get one that is part of the extension cord.

Placement Ideas

I've talked about many of the things that go into selecting a nice site for your pond, but not all ponds are the same. Let's get more specific about which type of pond looks best where.

Container gardens look great on patios and decks. They are easy to build and design in a style that matches your patio. How about the less obvious places? How about a whiskey barrel in the corner of your vegetable garden? Or in a flower bed in your yard? You can have several of these little water features in different styles at various spots in your garden.

Medium ponds add a "bigger" effect to your yard and cannot easily be moved. Corners and edges of the yard are nice places for them, and close to the house is very nice, too. It is especially pleasant to build a deck or patio next to your pond or to place it next to an existing patio. If you are putting in a swimming pool, a pond with fish nearby looks great.

Big ponds call for the most planning and may require contractor assistance. If you have a natural source of water, a spring or stream, a large earth-bottomed pond may be possible. For such a large project, I recommend that you work with a professional right from the start, including site selection.

Putting your pond near a window allows you to enjoy it any time of the day.

Part 3

The Pre-Formed Pond

You have probably seen pre-formed ponds at your local nursery and home improvement center. They might look like kiddie swimming pools, except they are usually rigid black plastic. They come in a variety of sizes, and you can even put several of them together. These small containers make good starter ponds for beginners. Let's go through the steps for installing this type of pond.

Lay It Out

I talked about pond placement earlier, so you already have a good idea of where you want to put your pond. With pre-formed ponds you have the luxury of changing your mind. Now that you have your pond shell, you can set it in different places in your yard, just like moving around a piece of furniture.

Pre-formed ponds are easy to buy, easy to place.

Once you have found the perfect place, start to think about how you are going to make the pond level. Also start to think about the landscaping around your pond. While you will do that after the pond is installed, you need to think about it beforehand. Why? Because small ponds look really goofy if they are just stuck out in the middle of the yard with nothing around them. Ponds are supposed to be a part of the natural landscape.

Pre-formed and other small ponds look best with some type of a natural background behind them. Shrubs and even flowering plants that grow very tall look very nice behind a pond. You can layer the background of your pond with a combination of trees, shrubs, and flowering plants to make an attractive, natural site for your pond.

Unnatural Look

Every day I drive by a house with a little pond out in the front yard. The pond is smack in the middle of the yard. It is small and it has a ring of flat rocks around part of it; the rest has black pond liner showing. The only decoration is a family of faded plastic ducks. My apologies to the person who built it, but it looks really goofy. A pond is supposed to be a little slice of the natural world.

Do You have Shelves?

Many pre-formed ponds have shelves built into them. This makes digging the hole harder. You can work with this problem two ways: accommodate it, or ignore it. If your soil is very hard, try to dig your hole to match the contours of the pond. Do the best you can; it doesn't have to be perfect. If your soil is a little easier to work with, you can simply dig the hole out to the deepest part, and then fill in under the shelf.

Digging Required

There are two ways to work with pre-formed ponds. One is to simply place the pond on ground level. We will talk about this later. The second way is to sink it into the ground. The bad news is that this means digging.

Take heart, this will be easy. First you need to determine the size of the hole that you will be digging. Place your pre-formed pond exactly where you want it to be, then trace the outer edge on the ground. This is the outline of your future hole.

Pre-formed ponds have a lip on the edge. To make your pond turn out a little better, leave this lip just above ground level. This will prevent rain water from running into your pond.

Part 3

Above Ground

You can also use a pre-formed pond in an above-ground installation. Do you have a raised flower bed or other area that you would like to build up? A pre-formed pond will be just the thing.

However, when I say "above ground" I do not mean simply plopping it on the lawn like a kiddie pool. I mean you build up around the pond, rather than digging down. You will need plenty of dirt to fill in around the pond.

This is also a great place to use the concrete building blocks that are common in home improvement centers. You can build a little wall around your pond, up to the height of the top lip. Remember to leave some areas that you will fill back in with dirt. You will then have a nice place to plant flowers or shrubs around your pond.

If you are going for a more formal look, choose a round or square pre-formed pond. You could build up a nice wall with bricks around the pond. This would look great incorporated into a brick patio.

Digging the spot for a pre-formed pond is easy, and the ponds look good.

Fill

If your pond is raised, you can use topsoil to fill in around it. Take extra time to pack it well around the pond itself. You will probably be able to reach under any shelf to pack the dirt by hand.

Back Fill

Your hole is ready or your raised bed is ready. Now you're ready to put your pre-formed pond in place. Pour in enough coarse sand to form a 2-inch layer after you've tamped it down. This is the base for the pond. Set the pre-formed pond right on top of the sand.

You will need to pack dirt back around the sides to add support and insulation to the pond. If your pond is below ground level, use more sand to fill in around the edges of the pond. If your pond has shelves built in, this may be

Part 3

difficult. One way to cheat is to fill the space between the pond and the ground with as much sand as possible. Now turn your garden hose on the sand. Not too much water–just enough to get the sand to flow down to the bottom of the hole. You will need to repeat this process several times. Wait for the water in the hole to drain into the ground before you squirt in more. You want the sand to be well packed around the pond. If you use too much water you might just float the pond right out of the hole!

Installing the Filter

Don't forget your filter as you dig. Did you plan how the filter should be attached to this type of pond? The easiest way to incorporate your filter into these small ponds is to use a submersible pump. Place the pump into your pond. You may want to get an enclosure for your pump that will keep fish and weeds out of the pump's suction. You can buy one specifically for this purpose or make due with a small laundry basket that you overturn on top of the pump.

There are several benefits to using your pond as the sump for the pump. You can use your pump to make a small waterfall or fountain that goes back into your pond. Don't forget to plumb it through the filter, though.

Fountains add action to any pond.

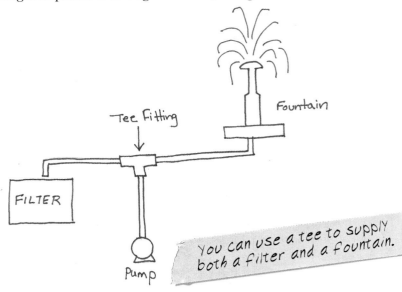

You can use a tee to supply both a filter and a fountain.

There are also pond filters that are designed to be submerged right in the pond. They are very good for the smaller ponds and would work well in your pre-formed pond. They are usually very similar to an above-the-ground filter, and you just sink the filter right into the pond. The pump is inside the filter box and the water will probably be drawn in through a small grate on the top. The only hassle I can see with this type of filter is that you will have to get wet to get it out and clean it. It will eventually get clogged up with debris and you'll have to rinse it out. That doesn't mean that these filters are bad. A submerged filter can be a practical solution for smaller water gardens. Just place it where you can reach it for cleaning.

Draining Your Pre-Formed Pond

For any water garden, it is a good idea to have a way to drain water. It is easy to build a drain into a pre-formed pond. You can use a bulkhead fitting to place a drain in the bottom. To install a bulkhead fitting in a rigid plastic pond, first mark with a pencil a circle that is just large enough to pass the bulkhead fitting through. Check it over a couple of times before you make any cuts that you cannot undo.

Carefully cut through the plastic with an Exacto knife or razor knife. You probably won't be able to make the cut completely through on the first go around. Just work carefully on the cut until you are through the plastic. Remember that you can always trim the edges and make the hole a bit bigger later.

Installing the bulkhead fitting is a cinch. Just tighten up the fitting to prevent any leakage. Bulkhead fittings have a threaded internal section that will allow you to screw in a piece of pipe. You will then connect a valve to this piece of pipe, and you have a drain.

Sumps

A sump is any low-lying place that receives drainage. If your pond is the sump for your pump, it means the water coming out of your pump drains directly into the pond. Since your pump is pumping filtered water, that's OK.

Suck It Out!

There is a way to avoid the whole drain issue that works well, especially in smaller ponds. You can use your submersible pump to drain out the water by diverting the flow from the pump to a suitable outlet. You can add an extra length of tubing to the pump outlet and point it wherever you please. If the plants around the pond need some watering, just use your pond water on them. Otherwise, direct the water away from the pond. If your pump is small, it might take a while to drain out your whole pond this way. Also remember that it is usually bad to run a pump dry (no water in it), so if you walk away while it is draining your pond, don't forget to check back now and again.

Part 3

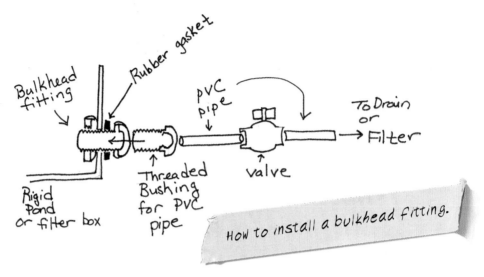

How to install a bulkhead fitting.

Add Some Air

Aeration may be more of a problem for smaller ponds because you may decide that you don't want to build a waterfall. No problem with that—you just may notice that in warm weather you see your fish up at the top trying to get a little more air. You can add a small fountain or an airstone to the pond to give the fish some relief.

There are many fountain kits available for small ponds that would work really well in a pre-formed pond. They are not too expensive, either. The kit will come with a small pump and a little fountain head to jet the water up into the air.

A small aquarium air pump and airstone will also work well. They are not designed to be outdoors, but I haven't had much trouble using them outside if they are covered up with an upside-down flower pot or other container to keep them out of the rain. You can easily hide one at the edge of your pond.

Final Landscaping

The most common mistake folks make with small ponds is finishing them off by putting a ring of rocks around the edge and calling it finished. If the ring of rocks doesn't fit with your existing landscaping, however, it can make the pond look out of place and too contrived. Try using very large rocks on the back of the pond, and taper them off to the front, which has no rocks at all.

Small ponds look best when they are tucked into your existing landscaping, just as if they were always there. Planting interesting bushes and plants around the edge to accent the pond will complete your look. It is always a good idea to look at gardening picture books to get ideas for completing your look.

A ring of rocks has become the "standard" pond edging.

Part 3

The Big Dig—Building a Liner Pond

Plastic liner materials have made garden pond-keeping much more accessible to the average gardener. Before they were developed, concrete was the material of choice, but concrete is expensive, hard to work with, very permanent, and not very well suited to cold climates. Hooray for liners!

Liner ponds can be small, but they can also be very large. You are limited only by the size of your yard and your budget. In this chapter I want to explain the basic steps required for liner pond construction. But let's not stop there. I will also talk about some of the pitfalls and mistakes that many people make with liner ponds, so that you know about them ahead of time.

Flexible liner ponds give you much more freedom when designing a pond.

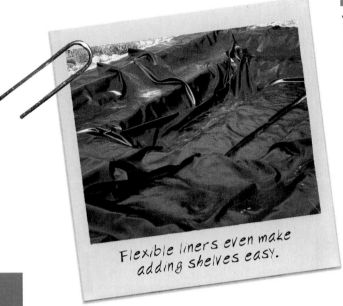

Flexible liners even make adding shelves easy.

Liner Materials

There are several types of liners available for pond construction. You may also be tempted to use some non-standard materials that are common at the home improvement warehouse stores, and I'll talk about those, too.

PVC

PVC is polyvinyl chloride, a strong material that is commonly used as piping. Swimming pool liners are made of PVC. It is usually available in 20-mil or 30-mil thickness. (A mil is a unit of measure; one mil is one 100th of an inch.) The advantages of PVC liner are that it is fairly inexpensive and readily available. You will see it included in some of the liner pond kits that are offered for sale.

I once built a pond with an old swimming pool liner. I simply called a pool installer in the spring when he would be making all of his liner changes and asked for a used liner. He gladly gave it away. You can't beat free! But I also assumed some risk in acquiring this liner. Some pool liner materials are treated with algicides and fungicides during the manufacturing process, and these can be harmful to fish. Since the liner was used, I took a chance that most of this stuff had already leached out of the liner. I washed the liner well before I installed it and let the pond sit for a few weeks before introducing any fish.

The other downside of a pool liner is the bright blue color. Black is the usual choice for a pond liner because it's easier to see the fish against a dark background and the black hides some of the folds and algal growth. However, my bright blue liner soon was a nice dark green from the algae. So much for algicide in the liner!

PVC is OK when used for smaller ponds and for projects that you may not want to last for a long time. The problem is PVC does not hold up well to ultraviolet light, and the sun provides plenty. Some PVC liner makers say their product can last ten years. Less expensive liners will have a three- to five-year life.

To extend the life of your PVC liner, make sure as much liner as possible is covered when it is above the water line. Use rocks, gravel, or sod to give good coverage. I used rocks all along the sides of my pond to cover the liner. Let the rocks hang over slightly to shade the inside edge. Water gives some protection against UV rays, and algae will soon take care of the rest.

Over time these liners become brittle and may develop some small leaks. My bright blue pool liner developed a few leaks in its third year. I was able to find them and patch them with an off-the-shelf swimming pool repair kit. The pond was just fine for the next two years. I eventually moved to a new home, but the last time I drove by my old place, the pond was still there.

Blue is a great color, but not always good for ponds.

I recommend new PVC liners for smaller projects and less permanent ones. I also think a used pool liner is all right as long as you really know its limitations on life span and don't object to the blue color.

Polyethylene

Polyethylene is a strong plastic material that is now available as a pond liner. Polyethylene sheet is also a common item at your local home improvement store, but you usually find it in the paint section as a drop cloth. This stuff is not suitable as a pond liner at all. It gets very unstable when exposed to lots of UV light and will become brittle in one short year. Make sure you buy only the pond liner type, which has been formulated specifically for pond applications.

Pond-grade polyethylene is available in 20- and 30-mil thicknesses. I do not have experience with this material, but the price seems reasonable. Make sure you buy your polyethylene liner from a reputable supplier who will offer you a warranty on the life of the liner.

An EPDM liner is the best, but it is more expensive than other liners.

EPDM Problems

please be careful to make sure the EPDM liner that you buy is fish-grade pond material. EPDM liners can be used as roofing materials and in landfill containment. Liners for these applications have probably been treated with fungicides and other chemicals that can harm your fish and plants.

Part 3

EPDM

EPDM (ethylene-propylene rubber) is the best liner material your money can buy. It is thicker than most pond liners, at 40 to 60 mils. It is also a more rubbery (as in stretchy) plastic, which adds to its life and usefulness. It will stretch around a rock or obstacle in the ground instead of tearing.

But there is bad news. As with all things of the highest quality, it is more expensive. You can expect to pay twice as much for an EPDM liner as you would for PVC. The long life of 20-plus years more than makes up for the up-front cost, however; so if you are building a pond that is meant to last, go with EPDM.

Other Liners

There are a few other liner materials available. One of these is Permalon, a multi-layered material that was developed for landfill use. I know a few folks who have used this material and like it, although they say it is a little more rigid and harder to form than more common liner materials.

When you look for liner materials and want to think about using something new, ask around. Find out who has used it and how they liked working with it. It is also important to find out how it is holding up over time.

I don't really recommend improvising too much with your liner. Stick with materials designed for the use intended. Plastic that was not made to contain living creatures may not be good for them. Playing safe will save you grief in the long run.

Comparison Shopping

You will find liners sold in a few different ways.

Liners may be sold in linear feet from a roll. This means that each foot taken off the roll costs a certain amount. If the roll is 5 feet wide, one linear foot of that liner is one foot long and 5 feet wide.

Liners may be sold in precut sizes for a flat price. An example would be a liner that is 15 feet by 12 feet for $120.

Liners may be sold by the square foot. A square foot is just what it says: a square that is a foot long on each of its four sides. You must specify the total width and the total length of the liner as a whole even though you will be paying by the individual square foot. There may be some limitations on the maximum length and width available, depending on what the supplier has in stock or what the manufacturer can make.

Under the Liner

To protect the liner from the bare dirt, you will need to put something under it. There are commercially available materials for this, but you can also use old carpeting or newspapers as underlay. If you are going all-out with a big project, spend a little extra to get the commercial stuff. It lasts longer and is designed specifically to protect your liner.

Here is a good way to figure out if you are getting your liner at the best price. No matter which of the above methods is used to price the liner, calculate the cost by dollars per square foot. Here is an example: You need a 10 x 15-foot liner for a stream bed you want to make. One dealer is selling a precut 12 x 15-foot liner for $120 dollars. Multiplying 12 times 15 gives you the total square footage of the liner, which is 180 square feet. Now divide 120 by 180 and you find out that the liner costs 67 cents per square foot. Seems OK.

What if another dealer is selling pieces from a 12-foot-wide roll for $7.20 a linear foot? You will need to buy 15 linear feet of the liner and will pay $108. You can already see that this is a better deal for the total cost. But let's finish the calculation anyway. You have 180 square feet for $108. That works out to 60 cents per square foot. Certainly a better deal.

But remember that you really wanted a 10-foot by 15-foot liner and will end up cutting the other 2 feet off. Your last place to shop will sell you your exact size liner for 70 cents a square foot. Hey, that is the highest price, isn't it? You now multiply 10 times 15 and get 150 square feet of liner. That comes out to $105. Are you surprised? Your lowest total cost had the highest cost per square foot!

By calculating both total cost and the cost per square foot, you can be a super comparison shopper.

Preparing the Site

The first step, of course, is deciding where to put the pond. You have already considered your elevations and how the pond will fit into your landscape. You are also probably sure about the size.

Now is a good time to get out your sketch pad and do some drawings of the area. You don't have to be an artist–this is just to help you make a sensible layout. You will need to lay out the entire project. Think about the plumbing, drains, filter box location, and your stream or waterfall (if you are building one). First do a bird's eye view.

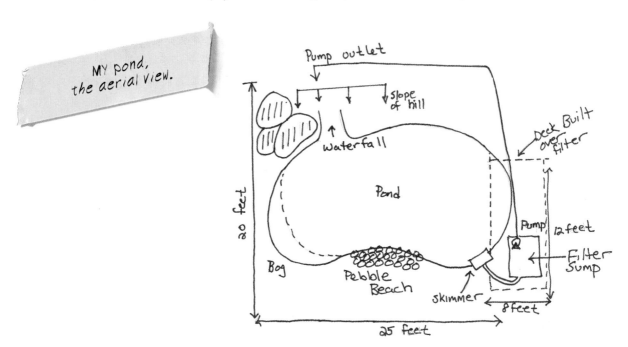

Then you'll need to sketch some of your details. Start using side views to help you visualize more and more details. You already know what your filter and other hardware look like, and you can use their sizes to plan their placement.

Stumped on the Sump?

The larger your pond, the larger the filter. One of the best ways to conceal a large filter system is to sink it into the ground along with your pond. The very best arrangement is to place the sump on the downhill side of your pond. Let gravity do its thing.

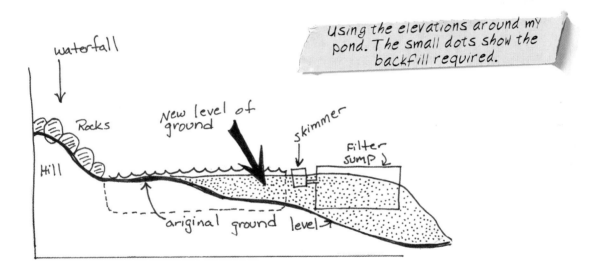

I think it is best to work from high to low when planning your pond and all its plumbing. If you have a perfectly flat site, you can still let gravity work for you. When I dug my last pond I made the lay of the land work for me. My drawing showed me where I'd need to fill in with dirt, and I needed a lot of dirt to raise the elevations for the pond. Where was I going to get all this dirt? The neat thing is, you will have plenty of dirt from the pond excavation. Why not plan from the start to use it up? Thus the value of your sketches.

Don't forget that your sump is also in the ground. Build a lip around it to divert rain water and include a large drain pipe, at least 4 inches in diameter, to drain any water that accumulates in the sump. Inside the sump, use concrete blocks to place your pump above the bottom of the sump to keep it from getting wet.

Simple shapes are easiest to make, but liners allow you tremendous flexibility

The Shape of Your Pond

The nice thing about liner ponds is that you can make more natural pond shapes. You simply dig the hole any shape you want and then line it with liner material. One neat way to play with shape ideas is to take out an old garden hose and use it to lay out a shape on the ground. You could also use a string or rope the same way.

Now, don't get the idea that you cannot have sharp corners and geometric shapes with liner ponds. Liners work very well in a formal pond where you use right angles and brickwork to raise the pond slightly off the ground. I'll talk about building this way a little later. The sides of your pond will work best if you can dig straight down. You can easily step into the pond this way, and it discourages predators.

Depth

The depth of your pond will depend on your climate. You do not want your pond to freeze solid during the cold winter months, and deeper water is less likely to freeze. Of course, you always have the option to heat the pond or bring the fish indoors when the weather gets cold, but either option complicates your pond experience.

My pond's filter sump. I planned this one with a deck over the filter boxes.

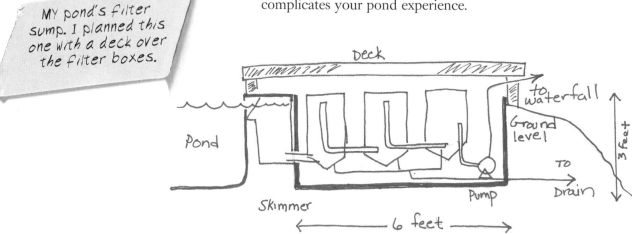

Even in warm climates there are advantages to deeper ponds. The water will be much cooler in summer if it is deeper. Think about when you go swimming–the water always feels colder around your feet. Larger fish, such as koi, also seem to grow better and be happier and healthier if they have deep water.

So what is reasonable? Plan on a depth of at least 18 inches, with a deeper section that goes down to 3 or 4 feet. Take the pond as deep as you think is safe for your home. If you are in a northern climate, a deep section will become very important. At 3 to 4 feet, you will probably not have freezing problems.

The depth of the pond is also important to water lilies. They like to have the crown of the plant 12 to 18 inches below the water's surface. When you take the height of the pot into account, 18 inches as your most shallow depth is the minimum.

Watch that Bottom!

Make your pond bottom flat, not curved. If the bottom is curved and you walk in the pond, you will probably land on your bottom! That means your deeper section should drop down like a shelf, with straight sides. (Make a point to remember where the shelf starts, or you'll still end up on your bottom.) Imagine an empty box sunk into the bottom of your pond. That's what your deep part should be like.

Pond Volume

A good estimate of the volume of your pond will help you pick the right filter and pump sizes. It is hard to exactly calculate the volume of an odd-shaped pond. Here is a method that will take a little time but is not too terribly difficult.

Take the sketch you already have done of your pond. Draw a rectangle around the pond, with the sides of the rectangle as close to each edge as possible. Now note on your sketch the approximate depths for each section.

Next, draw a grid over the whole pond at one- or 2-foot intervals. Count all of the squares that are completely inside the pond. In the sketch I made, my pond had 27 squares in the 3-foot depth area, 20 squares in the 2-foot depth, and 2 squares in the 1-foot depth. Now take all the squares that are only partially in the pond area and count each one as a half. Add it all up. In this example I had a total of 4 squares at 1-foot depth, 22 squares at 2 feet, and 31 squares at 3 feet.

That was easy! But here's the math part. I want to convert this whole thing into one-foot-by-one-foot-by-one foot cubes. For the one-foot depth, that's easy–there are four of them.

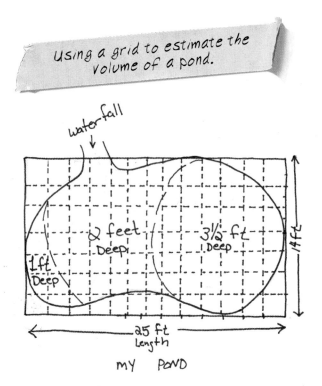

Using a grid to estimate the volume of a pond.

waterfall

2 feet Deep

3½ ft Deep

1ft Deep

4 ft

25 ft Length

MY POND

For the 2-foot depth, each square on my grid represents four one-foot cubes, so there are 88 of them. Finally, for the 3-foot depth each square represents six one-foot cubes–that's 186. Wow!

Now I have a total of 278 one-foot cubes. In other words, my pond is 278 cubic feet. But all the filters and pumps I've been looking at give their capacity in gallons of water, not cubic feet of pond. So I need to know how many gallons of water my 278-cubic-foot pond holds. Easy! I multiply by 7.5, and voila! My pond holds about 2,100 gallons. It's not exact, but it's close enough. Remember, each cubic foot of pond space can hold about 7.5 gallons of water.

Want to bypass the math? Buy a totalizing meter and measure the volume of water you need to fill the pond. The problem with this method is that you need to estimate the volume early so you can size your filter and other equipment at the beginning of the project. This means that you'll have to fill the pond and then drain it before you buy your equipment.

Volume Formulas

If your pond is rectangular or round, it is even easier to figure out the volume. You remember those formulas from your high school geometry class, right? Just in case you don't, here they are. Each measurement is in feet, and your answer will be in gallons.

Volume of a rectangle (gallons) = length x width x depth x 7.5

Volume of a circle (gallons) = Radius x radius x 3.14(pi) x depth x 7.5

How Much Liner Do You Need?

Your piece of liner will be a large rectangle that you will work with to line the hole you have prepared. But how big a piece do you need? First determine the length and width of your pond. This is the starting point. You then need to add extra liner for the depth of the pond. You will add two times the maximum depth to the length and width measurements.

For example, suppose your pond is a simple rectangle that's 10 feet by 12 feet. So far so good. On the deep end, the pond is 4 feet deep. So you take two times 4 feet, which is 8 feet, and add it to both the width and length. That now makes the liner you need 18 feet by 20 feet. You will also want to add one or two feet on each side for overlapping the edge. I think you should play it safe and add the two feet. That makes your liner 20 feet wide by 22 feet long.

Shelves require some extra computations to get a liner of proper size.

Here is the same idea in mathematical formulas:

Liner Width = pond width (at widest point) + (depth x 2) + 2 feet

Liner Length = pond length (at widest point) + (depth x 2) + 2 feet

You also need to think about any additional liner you will require if you are building in shelves on the sides of your pond to hold plants. Let's suppose your new pond is going to have a shelf on one side that is one foot wide and sits one foot below the top of the pond. You will have to add an additional foot to the pond liner to make up for the additional foot width of the shelf. For a pond with shelves on one side of the length and one side of the width, the formulas look like this:

Liner Width = width (across the pond) + shelf width #1 + shelf width #2 + (pond depth x 2) + 2 feet

Part 3

Before You Dig

Are you aware that your yard may be criss-crossed by water lines, electrical lines, sewage pipes, cable connections, and even pipelines? Do you want to cut through one of these and cause a local problem or even a major disaster? Before you dig, be sure you will not cut through something you will regret later. Call your water, power, gas, sewage, and cable companies so they can locate their lines for you. Even in remote areas you would be surprised at the problems that lie underground! Don't forget the septic tank and it's drainage!

You can rent almost any equipment you need to make pond digging easier.

Liner Length = length (across the pond)+ shelf width #1 + shelf width #2 + (pond depth x 2) + 2 feet.

If you have a shelf all the way around the pond, just double the depths and widths that the shelf takes up and add it to the simple liner measurement.

Now you have the total length and total width of your pond liner. But remember, I said liners are usually sold by the square foot. To calculate the square footage of your liner, just multiply the total width measurement by the total length measurement.

Can You Dig It?

You did all of your planning and you have the liner sitting in the garage. Hey, it's time to dig! There is no reason that you cannot dig the hole yourself. You are taking on a big job, though. The larger your pond, the more you will want to use some sort of equipment.

Renting Equipment

Many equipment rental centers have small tractors with a shovel on one end and a back-hoe on the other end. These are great tools for digging. It is fun to rent and do your own digging. Remember when you were a kid in the sandbox with your toy trucks? Doesn't it feel cool to dig with a real one? I have found that it does take quite a bit of time to become comfortable using the rental equipment. You will probably take a few hours just trying to figure out how to work all of the controls and dig effectively.

If you do decide to rent, ask for a complete demonstration before you bring anything home. Pay special attention to any safety advice. Plan on renting for a weekend, and see if you can get all of your digging and earth moving finished in two days.

Hire a Professional

I have found that if it will take you more than three or four days of rental time to complete the job, it may be less expensive to hire a guy with a truck to do the job for you.

You may find that most construction companies will not come out for a small job. However, there are many small contractors who can get your pond done in a very short amount of time. They already feel comfortable using digging equipment and can move an amazing amount of dirt in a short amount of time. What do you do with the dirt? Have your contractor move the dirt for you to a site you've chosen, or maybe you want the contractor to take it with them.

Get Out the Shovel

After you have done the bulk of the digging with a shovel or with heavy equipment, you will need to do some fine work with your shovel. You want to remove any rocks, tree roots, or other objects that stick out from the bottom or sides of the pond. You don't want any sharp objects that could pierce your liner.

Then you want to go over all of the excavation and refine the dig. Make the sides straight and smooth. Make your ledges flat and straight. You also want to make the bottom as flat as possible.

There are no shortcuts here. I have found that a certain amount of shovel and rake work is always required for the best results. The time you spend now will be well worth it later.

Finishing and Installing the Liner

Before you install the liner, place 2 to 4 inches of sand on the bottom of the pond. Rake it flat and compress the sand with a roller. You can also place a big piece of plywood over the bottom and walk on it to compress the sand. Place the underlay along the sides of the pond and on the ledges. You want to protect the sides of the liner from the bare ground.

Don't Forget the Pipes

You'll also need to lay in the pipes for your drain and any other plumbing that will be submerged. The best thing to do is to dig a trench in the bottom of the pond where the pipes will lie. Dig it deep enough that the pipes do not stick up. You want the bottom drain to be just slightly lower than the bottom. Lay in the pipes, and then cover them with sand. They don't need to be very deep under the sand, just covered. This will keep the bottom of the pond flat, with no lumps where the pipes are. Don't forget that the bottom drain will have a 90-degree bend where it comes up from the drain pipe.

Liners are tough, but don't abuse them as you install them.

Preparation

Order your liner and have it on-site before you start digging. This way you can make any last-minute adjustments to the pond dimensions in case the liner measurements do not work out the way you expected. Also, ask your supplier about what happens if it is the wrong size.

You are now ready to install the liner. You will find that the liner can be pretty heavy, especially if you are using EPDM. Ask a buddy for help or keep your pond party going through this stage of the process.

Most liners will have an inside and an outside, and this will be indicated on the liner. The outside, or back, of a liner may have some writing stamped on it or be slightly whitish. Place the backing facing the ground, on top of the underlay that you are using. The inside surface of the liner will be black. It may be hard to tell which side should be the inside. In this case, the part of the liner that is folded inside when you receive the liner is probably the inside part of the liner–the part that gets wet.

The liner will also have talc on it to keep it from sticking to itself. The talc is not harmful, but you should wash it off with a hose before you place the liner in the hole. Remember, the outside goes face down (facing the earth). The inside goes face-up and will form the inside of your pond.

You will have to play around with the liner placement to get it to fit just perfectly. Folding the liner in half works very well. Place the liner half way into the pond and move it around

Folds

Since a liner comes as a big, flat rectangular piece and your pond is not a flat rectangle, you will need to place some folds in the liner to make it fit. Just work the liner along the sides and make careful folds where it makes logical sense to do so. The folds will blend in and become invisible if you work at them carefully. Take care not to make really big folds. Use smaller, more frequent folds.

A liner party is a great way to get the help you need to put in a liner.

until it's just right. Then unfold. You want to make sure the liner makes good contact with all of the area you've excavated. Liners will stretch a little, but don't force the liner to do too much stretching or it will tear.

Installing Drains and Plumbing

You will need to cut a hole in your liner to install the drain. You may have also placed a skimmer or standpipe that will connect to your filter box; if so, you will need to cut an opening in the liner to install the skimmer. This is one place where I definitely recommend buying plumbing that is intended for liner ponds. It will be designed to go through the liner. The fixtures will also include a good way to seal the fitting around the liner to prevent any leaks at the place where the liner is cut.

Always use a good bulkhead fitting in any opening you make in your liner for plumbing. Spend the money, search far and wide, but get a real bulkhead fitting. Imagine what a royal pain in the posterior it would be to have a small leak in your liner from a bad joint!

Putting in the Drain

While you are at it, get a good bottom drain. Ask for installation instructions from the supplier. A drain will be very similar to a bulkhead fitting. Here are some general guidelines for installing a drain through a liner.

Part 3

A properly installed drain makes any pond easier to maintain.

You first need to lay in your drain piping under the liner. Attach the bottom portion of the drain fitting to your drain piping. Don't forget the gasket; use a little silicone sealer (aquarium grade, please) to hold it on the bottom seal ring.

Then lay your liner over the drain. Find the place where the lower half of the bottom drain has been installed underneath the liner. Feel around until you locate the six screw holes in the gasket and the rim of drain's lower half.

Take care and use an awl or punching tool to make a small hole through the liner. You want the diameter of the punched hole to be smaller than the screw you're going to use to attach the top half of the drain to the lower half. This will allow the rubber to make a tight seal against the screw.

Apply a light coating of silicone sealer to the liner in the circular area where the drain is located. Position the top gasket on the liner. Align the screw holes in the upper half of the bottom drain with the holes you punctured in your liner. Then attach the top to the bottom by carefully screwing them together. Make sure the flat surface of the top rim is flush with the liner. Do not over-tighten! The silicone sealer will act as a lubricant to keep the liner from twisting as you tighten. The liner should be firmly held between the two halves of the drain. The resulting compression of the gaskets against the liner makes a watertight seal. The sealed fitting should be level or slightly below the bottom of the pond. You will have a little depression that will help debris flow into the drain.

Now that the halves have been securely joined, you can carefully cut away the circular portion of the liner inside the drain. A razor knife will give you a clean cut. Trim the liner flush with the inside edges of the drain. You can put a bead of silicone sealer over the place where the liner and the inside surface meet.

Assemble the drain cover dome per the manufacturer's instructions. Except, despite what the instructions say, don't glue the dome in place. You will want to remove the cover dome for cleaning.

Part 3

Now for the skimmer. If you are using a swimming pool skimmer, it may be designed to install through a liner. For installing the skimmer, you should use a method very similar to the one you used for the bottom drain. You want to form something like a bulkhead fitting to seal the fixture to the liner. You can use gasket rubber from a home supply store to form a gasket on each side of the liner. Use silicone sealer between the gasket and the liner, then carefully use small screws to attach the skimmer fixture through the liner. Seal around the edge of the skimmer inlet with silicone sealer after you have attached it with the screws.

What About the Filter?

Where should you take water from the pond to run through your filter? This is the subject of some debate among pondologists. Some take in water from the bottom drain continuously, but this will add a lot of solids to the filter. I prefer to take in water from the top, skimming the surface. For a larger pond, I also add an intake from the middle level. I use the bottom drain to purge debris when I'm doing a routine clean-up.

If you're putting an intake pipe for your filter right at the surface of the water, you can lay the filter intake pipes on the surface. You'll need to dig a little trench leading up to the pond. Make it deep enough that the pipes will not be exposed after a heavy rain. If you take the water from midlevel, you'll have to plan for this before you lay in the liner, and the trench you dig will have to be a lot deeper to lay those pipes in. Remember, you're also then cutting more holes in the liner, and that means more bulkhead fittings. Set the filter intake into the liner just the way I described for the drain.

> ### Cover Domes
> The shape of the cover dome is designed to force debris and water to flow into the drain inlet. Therefore, keep potted plants, stones, or decorations away from the bottom drain so that water flow to the drain is not obstructed.

Don't use just rocks at the edge of the pond—try a bit of variety.

Finishing Up

You can fill your new pond before you place the edging materials. The weight of the water will help the liner settle into the hole. Remember to leave a small lip or, even better, a small trench around the pond to allow rain water to run around the pond, not into it. You will probably have to trim the liner edge–just leave enough to lap over the rim at least 6 to 8 inches.

Finishing the edge of a liner pond is pretty easy. You can tuck the liner edge under the stones, gravel, or other finishing materials. Finish up by smoothing the ground that has been disturbed. Plant your grass, bushes, and flowers that you planned for around the pond. You will enjoy your new water garden for years to come.

When You Want Pondzilla

Most of you will probably build a liner pond. Liners are perfect for medium-sized ponds and for irregularly shaped ponds. Liner ponds can also be very large. It is possible to buy a very large liner or even attach several liners to make one huge liner. Many of the materials that are used as pond liners are also used to line landfills. Landfills are big!

However, maybe you already have a concrete or earth pond. Most of the chapters in this book will apply to your pond anyway—so if you're just skimming in the bookstore, buy the book! Maybe you're just thinking about a big pond. Before you plunge in, I will point out a few things you need to consider.

Large ponds give you lots of room for plants and fish.

Concrete ponds are expensive to build and permanent.

You don't just drop concrete in a hole to build a concrete pond.

Maybe you have the money to get a contractor in to do it for you. In that case, this chapter will help you understand what you need to talk about with your contractor. I'll also tell you how to find someone you can work with.

Concrete Ponds

Building a concrete garden pond is very similar to building an in-ground concrete swimming pool. Now, if I were building with concrete, I would go whole hog and go with gunite construction. Gunite is a type of concrete used for swimming pools. The concrete is shot into place with a high-pressure nozzle, and a special formula is used that absorbs very little water. Any concrete must be reinforced with wire and rebar (those long thin bars you sometimes see lying around in little bundles at construction sites. The reinforcing skeleton will be built before the concrete is sprayed into place. All of the concrete should be sprayed on the same day to give you a solid, continuous structure. Spraying on different days creates weaknesses where the different layers join, and leaks can develop.

Concrete ponds need to have a very smooth surface if you are going to keep fish. If the surface is rough, the fish can get scratched when they brush against the pond. The scratches make it easy for infections to attack your poor little fishies.

Handling the Water In Concrete Ponds

Concrete is made of limestone, and limestone will make the water of your pond very basic. (Not basic as in fundamental, but basic as in the opposite of acidic.) The surface of the concrete must, therefore, be treated before it can be a happy

Part 3

home to your fish and plants. Before you fill the concrete pond, wash the surface with muriatic acid diluted one part acid to ten parts water. Be very careful when working with acids. They can burn your skin! Rinse the surface thoroughly and drain the pond.

The limestone in the concrete will also make the pH go up as it leaches out into the water. You must therefore add acid to lower the pH to 2 so that the acid will react with the limestone in the concrete (and eventually "use it all up"). You may need to add acid to the water several times to neutralize all the limestone in the surface of the concrete. You start by filling your pond with water. Get a good pH test kit and measure the pH every day. Add acid to bring the pH to 2. After you have added the acid, measure the pH every day. If the pH goes up over 8, add acid again until the pH is very low (2 again). Keep measuring the pH and adding acid every time the pH goes above 8. Eventually, the pH will not go up past 7. When you get to this point, drain the pond. Refill it, and let the water stand for one day before you measure the pH. If the pH has gone up to 8 or higher again, repeat the acid treatment. You want the water in the pond to stay at a pH close to 7 before you introduce plants and animals.

You can also coat the entire pond with neoprene rubber. There are several manufacturers that make coatings for concrete that are safe for fish and plants. You could also lay a liner into a concrete pond. Either method would be an excellent way to renovate an old concrete pond or swimming pool to make it pond-worthy.

Working With Concrete and Liners

There are times when it makes sense to work with both concrete and liners. For formal pond designs, concrete blocks and brick make a very nice way to construct square and rectangular ponds. You also can use blocks and bricks, as well as other materials, to raise the pond above ground level. Using a formal brick wall or landscaping blocks is also an excellent way to elevate one side of your pond to level it.

You could build a wall with the concrete blocks and bricks, using mortar. Place the structure on a firm footing of poured concrete, then bring the liner up to

Underpinings

Any heavy structure you put into or over your pond must have a solid concrete underpinning. A deck overhang, bridge, or stepping stone in your pond is really an interesting feature, but it is not especially safe. Consider not building one of these if you have children, or build railings to keep folks out of the water.

Part 3

the top of the wall. Finally, fold the liner over the top and use a few metal pins or small pieces of rebar to sink it into the block interior. You can then use a capping stone mortared in place to finish the top and cover the liner. You've now saved yourself the expense of having concrete sprayed in the interior of the blocks and bricks.

Earth Ponds

Here is another construction method that is not for the faint of heart or light of wallet. Unlike the other ponds I have discussed, in an earth pond there is no material between the ground and the water to hold the water back. You will need for the bare ground to hold in the water.

The common use for a pond like this is a farm pond for livestock. Earth ponds are also common for fish farming and large-scale aquatic plant production. Earth-bottomed ponds are usually much larger than your average water garden.

I highly recommend that you have a professional build an earth pond. There are just too many ways to make mistakes, and you could end up wasting a lot of time and even more money if you attempt this yourself. If you absolutely must try it on your own, please do lots of research first.

Several factors need to be present for this type of a pond to work well. First, your soil must be mostly clay. Clay is very heavy and naturally retains water. If the local soil is not adequate, it may be possible to bring in clay to line the bottom of the pond. The clay must be heavily compacted into the bottom of the pond to help it retain water. You could spend a lot of money just having the correct soil hauled in.

Earth ponds are prone to filling up with dirt over time. This requires you to get back in there with the digging equipment again. If you are building an earth pond, make additional plans to prevent dirt from erosion entering the pond. A good pond architect or contractor will explain how to do this.

A Stream is Nice

I have seen some fabulous examples of earth ponds built where there was an existing stream on the site. My pond club has a member who is an accomplished master of Japanese garden design and has created some wonderful koi ponds this way. The advantage if you have a site with a stream is that no filter will be needed at all due to the continuous supply of fresh water. However, you may not get the crystal-clear water that many people want. In Japan, koi are raised in mud-bottomed, murky ponds.

Part 3

Natural Ponds

I'm defining a natural pond as an earth-bottomed pond that already exists on your property. What can you do to make it more like a water garden? Let's talk about what you won't want to do first.

Be careful adding water plants that are unrestrained by pots or other containers. Many plants are very invasive and can take over the whole pond and eventually fill it in. Lotus and cattails are especially bad. You could attempt to dig them out, but you would likely have to dig every few years to keep them in check. You could use an herbicide to kill them, but you would likely also kill things you didn't intend to get rid of.

Earth ponds are much more difficult to build than you would imagine.

You could landscape the shores of the pond to make it more pleasing and add a few large pots of hardy water lilies. You can consider adding a few fish, but be careful that you are not releasing non-native species into your area. Make sure that any critters that you add are native, or they can wreak havoc on the ecology of your entire area—not just your pond.

Working With a Contractor

I have mentioned that you can find professionals to assist you with your large pond projects. You may have to consult a variety of pros for your specific interest, or you may

References

When you start looking for a contractor, take your time. I recommend that you call a few people who can do the job and ask them for price quotes. Then have them show you examples of their work and ask for references. Hopefully, you can visit other ponds they have built and chat with the proud owners. Don't be shy. Make sure that they were satisfied with all aspects of the project, and don't forget to ask if the project was completed on time and under budget.

Part 3

Consider hiring a contractor for a large pond or a concrete pond.

wish to find someone who can take a project from start to finish.

Most contractors will want to come out to see your site. This is a good time to talk with them, get a feel for what they can do, and make sure that you feel comfortable with them. Be sure to ask if they have ever dug a pond before. It is not a good idea to work with someone who hasn't.

Plan on being home on the day you have the work done. Don't be afraid to tell your contractor exactly what you want them to do. As the work progresses, add your suggestions. However, do remember that you've hired a professional. Add your suggestions about the pond, not the digging.

Moving the Waters

Moving water adds so much to your garden pond. The sound of water running over a waterfall or stream is extremely soothing. Waterfalls and streams also help add oxygen to the water for your fish. You will probably have a pump that pulls water out of your pond and through your filter. Why not get the water back into the pond in an interesting way?

Why a Waterfall?

There are some simple rules for how waterfalls work. The more water that falls and the farther it drops, the more energetic the waterfall. You really don't want to duplicate Niagara Falls in your backyard, for several reasons. First, your electric bill would be horrendous. Second, very vigorous splashing will

A small stream is easy to build and adds immensely to the pond.

Bigger Falls— More Equipment

If you want a really large and magnificent waterfall, your filter pump may not be able to supply enough flow. In this case, buy a separate pump for the waterfall or stream. Remember that if you wing it and just pick a pump based on flow rate not pressure, you will likely pay a higher electric bill or burn out your pump. Consult an experienced pond-builder for more information.

The higher the waterfall, the bigger the pump.

quickly empty your pond. Third, your fish will avoid the waterfall if it is too vigorous. Finally, you just don't need a lot of water flow to have a pleasing effect.

How High Should I Go?

I recently looked at the technical information for some of the more commonly used pond pumps and found that in most cases there is a foot or two of pumping power to spare. That means you can build a waterfall a foot or two high without having to get a more powerful pump. You have probably already zeroed in on a pump that you would like to use; just make sure you have a foot or two of pressure to spare for your waterfall or to power a stream.

Go With the Flow

Here is a rule of thumb for deciding how much flow you want for your waterfall. One hundred gallons per hour will give you about one inch of waterfall that is half an inch deep. If you want your waterfall to be 8 inches wide, you will want a flow of 800 gallons per hour for your pump, after considering losses to flowing through the pipes and fittings. This recommendation gives you a pleasing amount of water coming over the fall. It's hard to define "pleasing," but the idea is that you want a vigorous enough flow for it to seem like a good waterfall—not a little trickle.

By the way, half an inch high means the height of the water right at the top where it drops over the edge is half an inch. That doesn't mean it falls half an inch. In fact, once you pump the water over the edge of the waterfall, it doesn't take any extra energy to make it fall—gravity does that for you, so your water can fall as much as you like. The half-inch build-up at the lip of the falls gives it enough oomph to fall away from the edge and not just dribble over.

You could use less than 100 gallons per inch of width, but then the height of the water at the very lip of the fall will be less than half an inch. The less the flow, the more like a trickle the waterfall will be.

Design Ideas

You are going to be looking for a place to hide your filter system. Behind or inside a waterfall is a great place to put the filter boxes. However, you don't want to move your pump up above the level of your pond. The best way to think about this is that pumps push water, they don't suck it. If you are using a submersible pump, you can put it right in the pond and pump the water up to your filter system.

A waterfall does not have to be really high to be pleasing, but if you have a good site for some height, go ahead and use it. It is best to have your waterfall drop into a small pool before entering your pond; this avoids agitating the water in the pond too much.

You can establish several levels to make your waterfall more interesting. If you make each level a little wider, you will have an effect that makes the waterfall appear to be larger. You will also decrease the velocity of the water on each level, so that its final drop into the pond is not overly vigorous.

Rocks are Best

Waterfalls need rocks. If you have rocks in your yard, here is a good place to use them. However, you will probably have to buy rocks for your project. When you buy rocks for the pond itself, look for a few interesting ones for your waterfall or stream.

Use a Tee

The more water that flows over a waterfall, the farther the water will project out over the edge of the waterfall. You may have to play around with your flow rate to get the most pleasing effect. If it's projecting out too far, you can always put a T (tee) junction in the plumbing and direct part of the flow back to the pond. You will be able to adjust the flow to your liking this way.

Wow! Some water-falls are just stunning!

Part 3

Pre-Formed Waterfalls

Just like the pre-formed ponds, waterfall kits are also available. They are usually on the small side but can be used to make a small waterfall or a stream between two pre-formed ponds. You need to be creative with rocks to make a pre-formed waterfall look more natural. You can use aquarium-grade silicone sealer to glue rocks into place on the plastic waterfall. Be careful to place the stones so that water will not splash out of the waterfall. You would be amazed at how much water you can loose just by having a constant small splash.

Also have some small stones and gravel on hand to fill in the entire waterfall. Small stones and gravel are great filler in a waterway.

When you select any rocks for your pond, be sure to select those that have a low limestone content. Granite, slate, and shale are all interesting and don't have much limestone in them. When in doubt, do the soak test. Soak your rock in a bucket for a few days and test the pH of the water. If is high, over 8.0, you probably shouldn't use that rock. Be sure to measure the starting pH for reference. That way you'll know your tapwater isn't pH 8 and can definitely attribute the rise in pH to the rock.

Working With Pond Liner

You will need to use pond liner underneath your waterfall to contain the flow and direct it back to the pond. Liner is easy to cut to shape and form into your waterfall. The waterfall liner should overhang into the pond to prevent leakage. It is possible for the water to wick up behind the place where they overlap. You can avoid this by making sure that the pond liner is raised where the waterfall liner overlaps.

Stones

When selecting that special stone for the lip of the waterfall, think about what you would like the falls to look like. A flat stone will create a solid sheet of water falling over the edge. If you use many boulders, you will have a rapids effect.

The liner should overhang the sides of the waterfall by 8 to 12 inches on each side. If the waterfall has a gradual slope, it is a good idea to make the sides of the waterfall slightly raised to contain the water. Waterfalls are the most common place to have a leak. It can take lots of fiddling around to find and fix a waterfall leak.

Placing a drain in the bottom of the waterfall pool makes cleaning this area much more efficient. You can simply open the valve to the drain and hose the little pool out. Debris will collect in the bottom of the pool over time, and you will want a good way to remove it.

Placing Those Rocks

Remember the rocks and gravel that you bought? Now it's time to put them in place. Place the stones in the waterfall in an arrangement that you find pleasing. You will probably move them around before you settle on the arrangement you like best.

The part of the waterfall that the water drops from is called the weir. The weir is the hardest part of your waterfall to build. If you are using a flat stone, use a level to make sure the stone is placed perfectly flat. The water would not cover the whole surface evenly if the stone were not level. Water will also want to flow off of the sides of your weir. You can use silicone sealer to glue side stones onto the weir to keep your water where you want it–flowing off the front of the stone.

If you are using a pile of rocks as your weir, it will be a challenge to get the water to roll off the top of the rocks. You can use silicone sealer here to plug up the spaces between the rocks. This will force the water to roll over the stones.

Waterfalls add to the landscaping possibilities of any pond.

Building a Stream

Streams also add sound and motion to your pond. My old house had a pond with a small stream. The birds would drink and bathe in the stream. It was lots of fun to watch them splashing, and I got a kick out of their antics. On hot summer days, I am sure they were grateful for the drink.

Building a stream is a little easier than making a waterfall. It is really a waterfall lying on its side. The stream bed requires a slight slope toward your pond to

Streams need a liner just like the pond.

Part 3

keep the water moving. The steeper the slope and the more water pumped into it, the faster the stream will move.

It is also nice to add a small pool or two along the way as your stream heads toward your pond. A stream with some small pools will give you interesting locations to grow aquatic plants. Pools also give you the opportunity to place a clean-up drain. Just like the waterfall, debris will accumulate in the stream-bed. An intermediate pool and drain will allow you to hose it out periodically.

The Wilder, the Better

Get imaginative to make the stream more interesting. Add a large rock here and there. Remember, in the natural world streams are uneven and a little wild. Try not to make yours look like a water chute.

OK, this waterfall is probably a bit much for the typical pond.

Adding a stream also makes a natural biofilter for your pond. Theoretically, you could design the stream to make up the majority of your filter. You would simply add enough rock to provide the surface area required by your pond. All you would need is a solids removal chamber before sending the water to your stream.

Designing Your Stream

When laying out your stream, think about ways to make it look like a natural part of your landscape. Streams don't just pop up out of the ground. Use bushes or other features of your landscape to create the illusion that your stream winds on forever. Making the stream progressively wider as you go along gives the optical illusion that the stream is longer.

You need a gradual slope for your stream. What's neat is that this doesn't mean your yard must provide the needed slope. You can simply dig the stream bed progressively deeper as you approach the pond. Be sure to dig an edge on each side to contain the stream. Provide a slight lip to the edge to prevent rain water from running off into the stream.

Pond liner is used to contain the stream. After you have placed the liner, go ahead and add your rocks. Gravel makes good filler between rocks to conceal your liner. Keep the gravel shallow enough that you can give it a good hosing now and then to remove debris. Don't forget to lap the stream liner over your pond liner where the two meet. Prevent wicking by raising the lip where the stream enters the pond.

Fountains

Fountains are more typical in formal ponds. In Europe, elaborate fountains are common in town squares and on the estates of the wealthy. A fountain looks very nice in a formal garden, but it is, by definition, an artificial feature. A fountain will not have the natural look of a waterfall or stream.

For garden ponds, fountains are used to make an interesting display and add oxygen to the water. Fountain kits are available as stand-alone units that you can install in less than an hour. They come complete with a small pump and a fountain nozzle.

You can also use statues or other pottery to build your own fountain. All you have to do is incorporate a fountain kit into a statue or even a pile of rocks.

Fountains make a pond look nicer and also add needed aeration.

Part 3

The Garden Wall

Garden walls can be used as a dramatic backdrop to a formal pond. A traditional design that is attractive and interesting is to use a wall-mounted statue, usually a face that spits water into a semicircular fountain below. Ponds of this type are on the small side but make a nice place to display lilies. You can use a fence or wall as a creative backdrop for your garden pond. If you have a large pond, it will also give you some security. You could create your own fenced-in private escape. This would be especially nice if you live in the city and have a small backyard.

Be creative. Not all waterfalls have to come from rocks.

Most garden centers carry small fountains that you can use beside your pond. Many of them are made of concrete. Remember that concrete can increase the pH of your pond over time, but you can handle by keeping the fountain far enough away from the pond that rain water washing over it does not go back into the pond. You could also use clear polyurethane and paint it on the statue to seal it. Two coats of brush-on or spray polyurethane are plenty.

Back to the Plumbing

There's no way to get away from the plumbing. You need to get the water to your waterfall or other feature somehow, so let's bring up the plumbing issues that you may not have thought about.

Plumbing for Waterfalls

A lot of effort can go into building a waterfall. If it is a large one, it will require even more effort. I am sure you have done the calculations you need to make sure that the pump will be sending enough water to the fall, but what about the plumbing?

Every inch of pipe you need adds to the pressure loss in the total system. Because smaller diameter pipe has higher losses, the first thing you need to do is choose the correct diameter piping. If the waterfall is large, pay for larger piping to make your life easier later on.

Think carefully about where you put the plumbing. My preference is to place it where you can get to it later without taking the whole waterfall apart. Definitely bury it to get it out of sight,

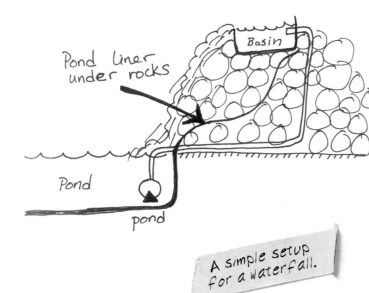

Pond liner under rocks

Basin

Pond

pond

A simple setup for a waterfall.

but you'll have to decide how much work you are willing to do to dig the piping up later, if need be.

One possible way to plumb a small waterfall is to use a submerged pump and tubing to deliver the water to the top of the waterfall. In this case a small plastic pan is used to make a small pool at the top of the waterfall. If the water just sprayed out of the pipe, the flow down the rocks would be less satisfying than when the pan is used. The pan produces a nice weir to spread the water out to make a good flow down the rocks. You may be able to purchase a pan like this, or you can build one yourself. The tubing for this type of waterfall is underneath the rocks of the waterfall. The tube is placed to the side of the waterfall and is covered with the same rocks used to make the waterfall. In this case, all you have to do is move a few rocks to get to the piping.

Plumbing for Streams

Plumbing a stream is easier. You still don't want to take the stream bed apart to get to the plumbing, so just bury it alongside the stream—and don't forget where you put it. Find an unobtrusive way to mark the pipeline. It won't be fun to have to dig up the whole area looking for your lost piping.

Plumbing for Fountains

There's not too much to say here. I think it is best to use a submersible pump for a fountain, and the plumbing simply comes up from the water underneath the fountain. Even if your fountain is placed to the side of the pond, it is a simple matter to conceal the plumbing at the edge of the pond.

Plumbing the Garden Wall

To make a garden wall look good, you definitely do not want to see the plumbing. Your only option is to go behind the wall. If you have a brick wall, you can use a masonry drill to make a small hole through the wall. You can pass the plumbing through the wall and up to the fountain. Since you will not have a liner in this sort of display, you need the stream of water to shoot out away from the wall and into the pool below. You may have to play around a while to get the desired effect. Even though it may look alright at the beginning to let a little water dribble down the wall, later the wall will become discolored from the constant moisture and perhaps become coated with algae. You need to keep the wall dry to preserve its beauty and its structural integrity.

Part 3

Cycling Your Pond

This chapter is not about bicycles or seasonal cycles or recycling or the cycles of the moon or the great cycle of life. It is, however, probably the most important thing you need to know to keep your pond healthy. Mother Nature, you see, is really wonderful. There is a natural system that works to keep the water in your pond clean and safe for your fish. It is called the nitrogen cycle.

The Nitrogen Cycle

Have you ever thought about what it is like to be a fish? You swim, you eat, and you poop–and you do it all in the same water. Gross! How is it possible to keep fish in a closed environment like a pond or aquarium? You would think that eventually they would be poisoned in their own waste. Well, this

Fish and plants are almost essential for a properly balanced pond.

Whew! Ammonia!

You have probably encountered ammonia as a household cleaner. Ever take a whiff from that bottle? It's horrible and poisonous. It wouldn't take long for a pond full of fish to excrete so much ammonia that they are poisoned in their own waste. If you had too many fish and not enough water, this could get out of hand fast.

Fish + plants = balance. The equation for a nice pond.

could happen, if you were a careless, heartless pondologist. But I know you aren't. Now you'll find out how you can use the nitrogen cycle to your advantage and create a nice home for your fish.

Humans and fish both produce nitrogen waste in the form of ammonia. Nitrogen waste is a by-product of protein digestion. We all need protein to live, and we need a way to get rid of the excess nitrogen that results from its digestion. Our bodies convert the ammonia to urea that passes from the body as urine, but fish excrete most of their ammonia directly from their gills into the water. They also release some as urine.

Bacteria to the Rescue

By now you may be wondering how any fish survive in a pond or aquarium. The answer is bacteria. A healthy pond or aquarium will establish a large population of bacteria that love to eat ammonia. There is also another type of bacteria that takes the waste from the ammonia-lovers and converts it again into a nontoxic form of nitrogen. Both of these types of bacteria live on surfaces inside the pond. They live on the rocks, the liner, and on plants, too. If you have a biofilter for your pond, you have simply provided lots of surface area for these guys to call home.

The problem is that when you build a new pond, the good bacteria have not had time to establish colonies in your pond. In other words, a sterile pond can be deadly to your fish. I know this might seem counterintuitive, but there are good bacteria and bad bacteria—and the good bacteria are absolutely essential for the survival of your fish. If you add too many fish too fast to a new pond,

Part 3

you are asking for disaster. You need to give the good bacteria time to colonize your system. They are all over everything anyway (isn't nature grand?) and will grow in response to the ammonia produced by your fish.

A Chemistry Lesson

Isn't this the best science project you ever worked on? There are all sorts of science to pond-keeping. Let's get more specific about the nitrogen cycle.

If you use a water test kit to measure the progress of the nitrogen cycle (which I definitely recommend), you will first see the ammonia level in the pond go up. You may actually see your fish become distressed as the level of ammonia increases. If you have added many fish or very large fish to a brand new pond, the ammonia level can get too high in just one day. This is why you are not going to add too many fish or very large fish to a new pond, right?

The bigger the fish, and the more of them, the more wastes in the water

What about all that ammonia? The first step in the nitrogen cycle is accomplished by bacteria called nitrosomonas. The nitrosomonas bacteria convert ammonia (NH_3) to nitrite (NO_2). It will take about a week for the nitrosomonas to multiply and start eating up the ammonia. The ammonia level starts to drop as the bacteria kick into high gear. Whew! Just in time.

We're not done yet. The problem is that nitrite is still toxic to fish, although it's not as bad as ammonia. Mother Nature to the rescue again! Another bacteria, called nitrobacter, will convert that nitrite (NO_2) to nitrate (NO_3). The good news is that nitrate is not harmful to your fish, unless it builds up to very high levels. You will take care of some of that with partial water changes. Plants also love all of the nitrogen chemicals, no matter how many oxygen atoms they have stuck to them, and will eat many of them up.

Nitrosomonas and nitrobacter are called aerobic bacteria. This means they need oxygen to do their job. It is easy to see from the chemical formula that they add oxygen to the

Part 3

Test Kits

A good investment for your pond is a test kit that you can use to measure the ammonia, nitrite, and nitrate levels in the water. The nitrate level is not critical to monitor because it is not toxic to your fish, but monitoring the ammonia and nitrite is very important. Use your tap water to become familiar with how your test kit works. You get to practice, and you can also measure the different water quality parameters of your water. You may find that your tap water is not great and is the source of high readings in your pond.

nitrogen. When the nitrosomas converts ammonia (NH_3) to nitrite (NO_2), you can see that oxygen has to be added. Converting nitrite (NO_2) to nitrate (NO_3) requires yet more oxygen.

Oxygen, Please

There is also another group of bacteria, called anaerobic, that do not use oxygen. Some of them cannot even live if there is oxygen present. Anaerobic bacteria can do some good and bad things in your pond. The good anaerobes have the potential to remove the nitrate. The bad guys use sulfur instead of oxygen. They make toxic hydrogen sulfide, which stinks like rotten eggs and can kill your fish. The potential harm far outweighs any benefit you could get from letting your pond go anaerobic. Your pond needs oxygen.

How to Cycle Your Pond

You will be rewarded by being patient with the way you add fish and plants to your pond. Let's assume that your pond is built, the water is in, and you are running the filter system. Most people build ponds in the spring, so we'll just assume that it is spring.

Temperature

An interesting tidbit: The beneficial bacteria do not function very well when the water temperature is below 55°F. They will be very slow to convert ammonia and nitrite and will die as the temperature goes lower. You will go through the nitrogen cycle every spring as your pond water warms up. This is a critical time for your fish.

For a new pond, I recommend that you just recirculate water through your filter system for two weeks before you begin to add any fish. You can use this time to make sure everything is working perfectly. Make sure that there are no leaks and that the water is at a stable pH. Imagine having to make small repairs if there are plants and fish already in the pond. If you find a leak later, you might have to remove all the fish. What a pain!

You can begin to add your plants to your pond when you are confident that there are no mechanical problems, such as leaks or filter problems. The more plants that you add before fish, the better. Plants will mitigate some of the effects of the nitrogen cycle when you add fish. It will take a little while for your new plants to make themselves at home and start growing. It is best to wait a month before you add any fish.

After you add fish–remember, just one or two–measure the ammonia and nitrite levels of the pond every day. You will first see ammonia and no nitrite. As the ammonia level gets higher, the nitrite levels will begin to register. The ammonia levels will start to drop off as the nitrite levels increase. If you decide to measure nitrate, you will see the nitrate levels slowly begin to rise as the nitrite levels fall. You do not need to monitor the nitrate levels, but do keep monitoring until you see both ammonia and nitrite levels fall to zero.

In a very large pond with only one or two small fish, you may not be able to measure the ammonia or nitrite levels at all. However, your pond still needs time to grow beneficial bacteria, so you still need to be patient. As you add more fish, or if you add a large fish, the ammonia levels may rise again as more bacteria grow to deal with the additional ammonia, but the spike should not last very long. It is best to put more fish in your pond one at a time, and don't ever put in too many. Even comet goldfish grow large very quickly, and you could end up with too many fish for your system to handle.

Cycling Problems

There can be problems as you cycle your pond. Maybe you weren't patient enough. Maybe you over-estimated how many fish you could add at one time. You can also see problems if you have moved fish to a temporary pond where there is no filter or you have a new filter. (Remember, a

Comets First

If you absolutely can't wait and have been admiring a special fish, go ahead and buy one. Just one. If you're looking at small fish and you have a pretty big pond, you can get away with three or four at the most. I recommend that you buy some small comet goldfish to start cycling your pond. Comet goldfish are very common in pet stores and are usually sold as feeder fish. They are cheap, too! They grow to be very sporty 10-inch fish and are really nice pond fish.

Common goldfish make great first fish for a new pond.

Part 3

new filter does not yet have a thriving colony of good bacteria to deal with ammonia and nitrite.) I clean out my pond once a year and move all the fish to a kiddie pool so that I can drain the pond. I keep a close eye on the fish while they are in their temporary home to make sure they are not getting poisoned.

How do you know there is a problem? Two simple ways. The most accurate is to do tests for ammonia and nitrite. Measure it–this is the best way to know exactly the condition of your water.

Your fish will also tell you that they are not happy. Koi will jump for fun sometimes, but they will definitely jump if the water quality is very bad. It will seem as if they are trying to get out of the pool. They probably are.

Ammonia toxicity can also make the fish lethargic. Finally, the fish might start to flash repeatedly. Flashing is a common fish behavior. They may do it because they are itchy. They may also do it because their skin is very irritated by bad water quality or parasites. If you see many fish flashing, or one that flashes repeatedly, investigate the cause of the behavior.

Ammonia Fixes

A kiddie pool is a convenient place to put your fish during pond cleaning.

There are several things you can do to help your fish if you are experiencing high ammonia levels. When you have confirmed with your handy test kit that there is a problem, your immediate attention is needed. If the ammonia level is just creeping up a little, don't panic. You need some ammonia in the water for the good bacteria to start multiplying. Confirm that the level is too high before you take steps. Your test kit will indicate what level of ammonia is too high.

The most immediate and simple thing you can do is to change the water. If you have a well, just turn on the hose and let it rip. You may even see your fish get right into the stream of the hose for relief. Make sure you are adding good water to the pond, though, so you don't make your problem worse. If you have already determined that your local water needs to be treated before it goes into the pond, then do so.

Another option is to add a liquid ammonia remover such as Amquel. Amquel reacts with the ammonia to make it less toxic. You definitely do not want to rely on a product like this to solve a chronic ammonia problem, but it is an excellent first aid measure. Also consider putting Amquel in the bag or container that you use to bring your fish home. Especially with large koi, there could be more fish than water in the bag.

Zeolite

A second option is to use zeolite chips in your filter chamber. Zeolite is a mineral that absorbs ammonia from the water. It looks like white gravel but is porous and soaks up the ammonia molecules. It takes about one gram of zeolite to remove 1.5 milligrams of ammonia. Let me translate that for you. You will need 25 grams (0.13 lb.) of zeolite to remove 1 ppm [parts per million] of ammonia from 10 gallons of water. If you are keeping the fish in a 1,000-gallon pond and your test kit tells you your ammonia is 2 ppm too high, you'll need 5,000 grams of zeolite to get the ammonia level down to where it should be.

Zeolite will stop working when it has absorbed as much ammonia as it can hold. You can regenerate the spent zeolite by soaking it in a solution of salt and water, then rinsing it and drying it. You can probably get three or four uses from a batch. Do not regenerate it by adding salt to your pond because the zeolite then will let go of all that ammonia it was holding, leading to a major disaster.

Salt

Zeolite cannot bind ammonia very well in the presence of salt. If you have added salt to your pond and have an ammonia problem, zeolite will not work well for you. Use a liquid ammonia remover instead. Don't play mad scientist with your pond when cycling. The ammonia goes up so you put some zeolite in the filter box. The ammonia comes down, but now the nitrite is starting to go up, so you add some salt to the pond to help out with the nitrite. A couple of hours later the fish are starting to die. That salt just released all the ammonia from the zeolite!

Mesh laundry bags are excellent containers for zeolite. You can move the bags into your filter box as needed. When you go to a koi show you will probably see a little bag of white gravel in each tank. Now you know what it is and what it is used for.

Part 3

Ammonia and pH

To fix an ammonia problem you can lower the pH of the water to around 6.8. Ammonia is much more toxic at a high pH. If your pond pH has gone up past 8, ammonia can be especially toxic.

Nitrite Knock-outs

The nitrosomonas bacteria now have kicked in and are changing the ammonia to nitrite. Nitrite is still toxic to your fish, and the nitrobacter is now ready to do its job. However, it is going to take time for the second shift bacteria to colonize the filter and get busy with the nitrite. What can you do if the nitrite levels get too high in the meantime?

You are testing your water, right? OK, if the nitrite is too high, the best thing to do is change about 20 percent of the pond water. Resist the urge to toss in a lot of chemicals; changing water should be your first choice. You need some of the offending ammonia or nitrite present in the water for the good bacteria to live on as they multiply and colonize your pond. If you freak out and completely remove the bad stuff, you will just postpone the inevitable–a healthy, well-cycled pond.

Cycle your pond with a small fish load at first.

If the fish are looking a little stressed and nitrite is the culprit, the best thing to do is to add some salt to the pond. Regular non-iodized salt is fine. Salt makes the nitrite less toxic to the fish. Add one teaspoon of salt per gallon. You can use table salt, rock salt, or sea salt. I usually buy table salt in bulk from a warehouse club to get the best price. Make sure that you remove any zeolite before you add salt.

The Tortoise and the Hare

The nitrogen cycle will just take some time to start working in your pond. The temperature needs to be over 55°F, and some ammonia and some nitrite must be present to feed the growing bacteria. There is really nothing you can do to make it happen any faster than it will happen. Just keep testing the water every few days and let nature take its course.

Part 3

The best approach is to just go through the cycle with a small fish load, and you should have no problems at all. I have told you how to solve problems should they arise, but don't think you have to do anything just because you measure some ammonia and nitrite. Be sure that you have a problem before you act. You and your fish should cycle along just fine if you watch carefully and choose the simplest actions first.

Plants make pond cycling faster and more certain.

Part 3

Part Four
Plants and Fish

"Finally! The new fish are taking to the garden pond"

Plants In and Around the Pond

Here we are. You have built a beautiful water garden. It is full of clear, clean water. The filter is humming, the waterfall is gurgling. It is time to think about what you want to put into your garden. Many of you may want to keep only plants, with no fish, so I'll talk about plants first. Plant-only ponds can be very beautiful, and if you also want fish, you'll have an easier time cycling your pond if the plants are in and thriving. They will take up the ammonia that your fish produce and ease your filter into its job.

There are hundreds of plants that are great additions to your water garden, so it would be impossible to mention every one in this book. Instead, I will talk about the most common types and varieties and

Water lilies and ponds just go together well.

Vallisneria, often just called val, is an attractive oxygenating plant.

give you ideas about where to find more unusual species.

You will probably want to stock your pond with a variety of different plants. This will add to the textures and experience of the pond. You will want those that flower and those that add beautiful foliage. Submerged plants add interest as you gaze into the depths of the water. Floating plants dance on the surface—and make great little filters, too. Plants also become food for your fish.

Sinkers—Oxygenating Plants

Oxygenating plants live their lives submerged in the water. In strong light they liberate oxygen directly into the water. They can act as natural water softeners by reducing the mineral content of the water. They compete with free algae for nutrients and help eliminate algal blooms. For all these reasons, these are must-have plants for your water garden.

It is best to place those plants in a basket full of gravel to keep them anchored. You can use a small laundry or storage basket or a basket for water plants. You can attach the bunch of plants directly to the bottom of the container with a rubber band or a twist tie. I like to stick bunches of them in the rocks on the sides of the pond.

In warm climates, you can also try tropical submerged species in pots in your pond. These include *Vallisneria* species (val) and *Cryptocoryne* species (crypts), which are bottom-dwellers. They can also grow well in a slow-moving part of a stream bed. They are not able to withstand cold weather, so bring them in for the winter.

Koi Food

It is not unusual for pieces of submerged plants to break free and populate other parts of the pond. You may also find yourself removing them from your filter box from time to time as they get sucked in. Koi love to eat these guys, too, and you will probably have a very hard time keeping any in your pond if large koi are present.

Bunch Plants

These are the familiar aquarium plants you see everywhere, usually as foot-long bundles of bright green leafy stems. Though they are technically rooted, submerged plants, they grow

Part 4

toward the surface very rapidly and also break loose to float around the pond in large and small clumps. They are excellent oxygenators and are eaten by many fish.

√ Anacharis or elodea (usually *Egeria densa*) is the most common bunch plant that you will find. It can survive the winter outdoors if it doesn't get too cold. Anacharis has small green leaves that are compactly whorled around a brittle stem. The stem can break easily, but a new plant will grow. In very warm water, above 75°F, the plants may become lanky. It's an excellent choice for all water gardens.

√ Canadian pondweed (*Elodea canadensis*) is very similar to anacharis, except the leaves are not as long on the plant stems and curl under slightly. It is the northern cousin of anacharis and likes cool water (below 70°) for best growth.

√ Fanwort, usually Carolina fanwort (*Cabomba caroliniana*), is a southern submerged plant that likes warm waters. It has feathery, bright green foliage that has a fan shape. The plant will extend small white flowers to the surface of the water.

√ Hornwort, also called coontail or foxtail (*Ceratophyllum demersum*) looks similar to fanwort but has a compact flower that does not rise to the surface. It makes an excellent breeding area for fish. In the fall, the compact tips break off the plant and fall to the bottom of the pond to over-winter.

Floating Plants

These guys are very easy to care for because they just float around on the surface and hang their roots below them like some sort of jellyfish. These are excellent

Pondweed, Elodea and relatives, is easy to find and grows almost anywhere.

Carolina fanwort, Cabomba caroliniana.

Part 4

Water hyacinth, Eichhornia crassipes, is interesting but invasive.

plants for a "vegetable filter." They provide shade for the pond, hiding places for the critters, and are nutrient magnets. Many species are extremely prolific. You may find yourself removing wheelbarrow loads of them from your water garden; just add them to the compost heap. Never release these plants into native waters—they are just too invasive.

√ Fairy moss (*Azolla caroliniana*) is a delicate-looking floater that has bright green leaves that turn red in full sun and in the fall. Fairy moss has a little root cluster that drops into the water under each leaflet. They reproduce quickly and fish seem to find them distasteful, so they cover the surface in no time. A pool skimmer is an easy way to remove them from the pond. They are not winter-hardy but can be over-wintered indoors in a pan of water on a windowsill. Fairy moss really is a type of floating fern.

√ Water hyacinth (*Eichhornia crassipes*) has leaves with large bladders filled with air that keep them afloat. Water hyacinths have a large, hairy root system that drops far into the water below. They are excellent "vegetable filters." They reproduce by runners and are extremely prolific. In the pond, they may become a nuisance and clog up your filter. My koi always pulled the roots off, making a huge mess in the pond. Water hyacinths have a lovely bloom, but I have only had them bloom when they have occupied every available opening. Grow them in a container to encourage blooming. This is a great plant, but it is not winter-hardy and it's hard to get them to live all winter indoors. Don't buy a lot of water hyacinth, because one or two will quickly populate your whole pond.

√ Duckweed (*Lemna minor*) is one of the most familiar aquatic plants. It is seen as tiny bright green leaflets floating on top of the water almost like a green scum. This is a great little plant that drops a tiny little root into the water below the leaflets. It is winter-hardy in most U.S. climates, and fish love to eat it. Consider growing some away from the fish so you can keep a supply on hand, but actually it reproduces so fast during the summer that you will probably be skimming it off rather than trying to make it grow.

√ Water lettuce (*Pistia stratiotes*) is vaguely similar in appearance to water hyacinth, but with a velvety green leaf. Its growth habits and care are similar to those of hyacinths, but it does not produce a spectacular flower and lacks the air-filled bladders. Water lettuce may turn yellow in some ponds. Give yellowing plants a rest in a bucket full of water and fertilizer mix and return the plants to the pond when they are recovered. This plant seems to prefer partial shade. It also hates cold and will turn to mush after a frost. It is very difficult to over-winter indoors.

Water Lilies

Water lilies and lotus plants are the real plant show-stoppers for water gardens. Water lilies come in a vast variety of colors, sizes, and bloom styles. The mystical lotus also has plenty of varieties for the water gardener. Given proper care, these plants will be with you season after season.

Water lilies are species of the genus *Nymphaea*. There are two general types: hardy and tropical water lilies. Hardy lilies can spend the winter in your pond, but tropicals cannot unless you are in the South. Water lilies come from all over the world and are also highly hybridized, with new varieties coming onto the market every year. There are just too many to talk about in more than a general way in this book, but you can look at catalogs and gardening books devoted just to water lilies for more details. Look at pictures and visit your local plant nurseries to decide what lilies are right for your pond.

Native water lilies may over-winter in the southern states.

The most beautiful tropical lilies will have to be moved indoors in cold weather.

Part 4

Hardy lilies usually have smooth leaf margins and bloom only during the day.

Lilies and similar plants should be split and replanted on a regular basis.

Part 4

Annual Lilies

Many gardeners grow tropicals as annuals, which means they buy new ones every year. They will not survive a cold winter. There are day-blooming and night-blooming varieties, the night-bloomers being especially fragrant.

Hardy Water Lilies

These will be able to hibernate in your pond over the winter, as long as the rhizome does not freeze. The blooms will open during the day and close at night. Most blooms will last many days before dropping below the surface.

Tropical Treasures

You can tell the group of tropical water lilies from the hardy lilies by the way their leaves look and from the flowers. The leaves will be serrated on the edges, while hardy lilies have a smooth-edged leaf. The flowers of tropical lilies rise above the surface of the water, while those of hardy lilies generally float on the surface. Tropical water lilies make new tubers that can be stored over the winter. Many day-blooming tropical lilies also produce new plants by viviparous propagation, meaning they make little baby plants on their leaves. All you have to do is let the babies grow a few good roots, separate them from the mother plant, and put them in their own pot.

Show Me Your Rhizome

Water lilies require dirt to grow in, so they will have to be potted in your pond. Most mail order plants will

Planting a water lily.

Before replanting a lily, trim off most of the leaves.

come "bare root" (no dirt, just roots) and require planting. You may also purchase them potted and ready for your pond. You will also probably want to break up and repot your lilies at some point.

To understand how to pot a water lily, you need to know some plant anatomy. Water lilies and lotus both have a tuberous root called the rhizome. Water lilies have different types of rhizomes, but they are similar in that every plant grows from a tuberous root structure. Potting all is similar.

First, you need to select a pot for your lily. There are a variety of options, and most will work just fine. Many garden supply stores carry baskets for water plants. I also like to use old-fashioned red clay pots for lilies, although a vigorous lily can burst right through a clay pot. Clay pots are inexpensive and easy to work with. You can also look for the type of clay pot used for orchids; these have openings on the sides that will let water flow around your lily, like the baskets. The size of the pot depends on the lily variety. For large plants, a five-gallon pot is fine. One gallon will be just right for smaller plants.

Part 4

Soil Problems

Some commercial potting soils may not work well for aquatic plants. Potting soils with a lot of peat moss will tend to float away and tint your water brown. Look for commercial soils that are specifically for aquatic plants. Heavy loam and clay can also be used, just be sure there are no yard chemicals in the soil.

Before potting, you'll want to trim the plant using pruning shears or a sharp knife. Cut off any dead, brown, or nasty-looking bits of rhizome. It is OK to expose the white inner part of the rhizome. You can then divide your rhizome if you wish. Sections of 2 to 3 inches are about right. Be sure to keep an "eye" or obvious leaf growth on each section. Trim off any roots and leaves that are old, brown, or decayed looking. It is all right to remove any developed leaves that look too old. You want to keep unfurled and very new leaves on your plant.

Fill the bottom of your pot with some coarse gravel then add potting soil until the pot is three-quarters full. You can use soil from your yard or special aquatic plant soil. I like to use my local soil because of its high clay content. Lilies love it. Place three or four aquatic plant fertilizer tabs in the container with the soil.

If the rhizome is a horizontal grower, place the cut end close to the edge of your pot. This way the growing end has plenty of room to spread across the pot. For the clumping types, place the rhizome in the center of the pot. Spread any roots out on the top of the soil. Cover the roots and rhizome with your soil mix. The "eye" or leaves should be facing up and left uncovered. Finally, place a layer of coarse gravel over the soil. The gravel will help hold the plant down and keep smaller fish out of it. You can now place your lily in the pond.

The Lotus Position

I just love lotus plants. The leaves are as big as dinner plates, and water beads up and runs off them as if they were wax. The flowers are just spectacular and come in shades of white, pink, and yellow. The center of the flower matures into an interesting pod full of seeds and when dried looks very interesting in flower arrangements. Lotus will not come back if the tuber is allowed to freeze. All these plants belong in the genus *Nelumbo*.

Planting a Lotus

Planting a lotus is a little different from planting a water lily. Lotus are usually large and very vigorous plants. They have horizontally growing tubers that will spread very quickly, so a shallow, wide pot is the best for lotus. I also prefer to use a closed container for growing lotus plants. That means no hole in the bottom of the pot. With a closed container you can raise the lip of the pot above the surface of the water. If you have large fish, this keeps them from digging up the plant while still ensuring that the water level will be over the roots of the plant. If the pot had holes in the bottom, the water level in the pot would be the same as in the pond–too low for the lotus. Large lotus plants require large pots 3 to 4 feet in diameter. The dwarf varieties should be planted in bushel-size containers.

Lotus require only a few inches of water on top of their roots. They are also heavy feeders and like lots of fertilizer once they get going. Lotus do best with more fertilizer than other plants–a few tabs every month in the growing season. If the pot has no hole in the bottom, the fertilizer does not get out into the pond and provoke an algal bloom. You just have to remember to water the lotus frequently to keep the required amount of water over the top of its roots. You can keep lotus out of the pond this way, too.

Nelumbo lutea, the native water lotus, is widespread in the U.S.

To plant your tuber, place coarse gravel on the bottom of the container–just enough to cover the bottom is fine. Place five or six plant fertilizer tabs around the bottom of the pot, then add 4 to 5 inches of soil to the pot. Your lotus tuber will probably have a tip where a few roots or a new leaf or two are beginning to sprout. Place the tuber near the edge of the pot, with the leaf pointing up. Place a flat stone on the tuber to hold it in place.

Gently fill the container with water so that there are 2 to 3 inches covering the tuber. Place your tub in a protected place where it can get plenty of sun. The tuber will not be happy and may even die if it is too cold. Your lotus will really start to grow once the temperature is above 70° outside during the day. Once the plant has grown several leaves, cover the tuber with soil, taking care not to damage the growing tip. You may add a very light layer of gravel on top if you like, to keep the fish away. Once the weather is warm and your lotus is growing well, you can place it in your pond.

Amazon giant water lilies, Victoria, often are seen in public gardens.

Propagating Lilies and Lotus

Propagation means creating new plants from your old plants. In general, this is pretty easy with water plants. You will be amazed at how vigorously most water plants grow. That means you will have to eventually repot all your plants. The neat part is that you will probably be able to have new plants from your old favorites.

Propagating new plants from old plants is amazingly easy. First you need a nice sharp knife such as a kitchen knife or gardening shears. The best time for dividing your plants is in the very early spring, before or just after the plants have begun to wake up. Here are the very easy steps:

√ Take the plant out of its pot.

√ Wash the majority of soil away from the roots.

√ With lilies, cut the rhizome into pieces. Each piece needs to have a growth "eye" and its nearby roots. On clumping types, saw through the clump in two or three places. You will see new tuber-like bulbs on the main bulb. Cut them off to make new plants.

√ Repot the new sections and return them to your pond or, even better, give them to your pond friends.

√ Wait to divide lotus tubers until spring.

Care and Feeding

Water lilies and lotus are very easy to care for. You need to give them a few fertilizer tabs at the beginning of each pond season and when you replant them. To keep them blooming

Off With the Old

Lilies and lotus naturally renew their leaves and flowers. Remove old worn-out leaves to encourage the growth of new healthy leaves. I also recommend removing the stems of withered flowers. That way, the plant will use its energy to make new flowers instead of making seeds in the finished flowers. However, lotus seed pods are really neat and you may want to let them develop. If not, just nip them off when the lotus has dropped all the petals from the flower.

Part 4

all season, add a plant tab or two each month. Tropical water lilies should be fed until the middle of August.

If you are continually getting algal blooms, stop feeding your lilies and only fertilize them when they seem to slow down in making new blooms. Lotuses like more fertilizer, so give them three or four tabs a month. You will not have to worry about too much fertilizer in your pond if you keep your lotus pots above the level of the pond water.

If you see your plants turning yellow immediately after a feeding, you may have added too much fertilizer. Fish the tabs out of the dirt and wait for the plants to recover before feeding again.

Life on the Edge

The plants at the shallow edges of your pond are called marginals. These plants like to get their feet wet, but just a little bit. You can creatively use marginal plants to customize the look of your pond. Everybody will probably keep lilies and other submerged or floating plants in their pond, but by selecting interesting and unusual marginal plants you can create a scene that is uniquely you.

Most marginal plants have very similar planting instructions. They have thick or tuberous roots. Plant the large varieties in large pots. Put some gravel in the bottom of the pot and use a loamy or clay soil. The best type of pot for marginals is a typical houseplant pot

Buttonbush is a shrub that will move into the margins of many ponds.

Nesting Grounds

Reeds and grasses make homes for wildlife in natural wetlands. Birds nest in them and they provide cover for animals in the water. Your grasses may attract some residents to your pond as well.

Cannas are terrestrial but adapt well to pond margins or even shallow water.

Dwarf papyrus, Cyperus, makes a nice backdrop.

with solid sides and holes in the bottom. I have also used the plastic pots that are designed for window boxes for my marginals.

Cannas

You may know these from your terrestrial garden. Cannas come in a variety of colors and sizes, and some have variegated foliage. They can be adapted to live as a marginal water plant. Plant cannas in five-gallon pots with rich potting soil covered with a fine layer of gravel. Use a regular pot with drainage holes in the bottom.

When you first plant them, keep your cannas out of your pond but water them very frequently. Two weeks later place them in the pond with the pot just out of the water. In another two weeks you can move them in deeper, with the pot 2 or 3 inches below the surface of the water.

Papyrus

Papyrus plants were used by the ancient Egyptians to make paper. The Egyptians relied on the Nile River for many of life's necessities, including the papyrus plant. Members of this genus, *Cyperus*, range in size from small to really huge. *Cyperus alternifolius*, the umbrella palm, is a small variety that grows to 12 to 36 inches high and resembles a palm tree. The big boys, *Cyperus giganteus* (Mexican papyrus) and *Cyperus papyrus* (giant papyrus or Egyptian paper reed), can grow to 15 feet!

Small varieties can be planted in five-gallon containers, but plan on 20-gallon pots for the large varieties. They are not winter-hardy but can be brought indoors for the winter.

Cattails

Cattails are common all over the United States. You have probably seen the long-leaved green plants with the brown fuzzy flower heads in roadside ditches. In the fall the fuzzy flowers turn to white fluff as the seeds begin to disperse. Cattails are an interesting and welcome addition to the water garden. Plant cattails in five-gallon pots in clay or loam soil. Submerge the pot 1 or 2 inches below the top of the water.

Typha latifolia is the common cattail found growing wild. It is a very tall plant, reaching 7 to 9 feet. Since these are so common, see if you can find them in a local waterway or ditch. They transplant like champs. The plant grows from a bulb-like root and spreads like wildfire once it's planted. It is so good at growing that I have had these cattails break open clay pots. My native cattails eventually took hold in the rocks on the sides of my pond. I was happy with them there, but you may not want them to take over this way.

Another hassle with tall plants is that the pots can blow over in a strong wind. *Typha angustifolia* has narrow leaves and is short, growing to around 4 feet tall. There is a miniature version for small ponds and containers, *Typha minima*, that only reaches a height of 12 to 18 inches. It has smaller flowers that look more like brown balls instead of the long tails found on other varieties. This mini can be planted in a one-gallon container.

Rushes, Reeds, and Grasses

I decided to lump all of these plants into one section because they look similar and have similar requirements. Most of these varieties have long green leaves that stand straight up from their pots. Use reeds, rushes, and grasses in your water garden to give an attractive background to other marginal plants.

Zebra rush, Scirpus tabernaemontani.

Arundo donax, also known as the giant rush or giant reed, is 3 to 8 feet tall and has a bamboo-like appearance with 3-inch-wide leaves. There is a variegated variety available that has nice white and green leaves. Since this is a large plant, it is best for larger ponds. Plant in clay soil and place in full sun at a depth of up to 6 inches.

Part 4

Sweet flag, Acorus, grows well in a pot in shallow water.

Butomus umbellatus is the pretty flowering rush. It has slender leaves that reach 2 to 4 feet tall. The flowers look like umbrellas with pink blooms.

Eleocharis montevidensis is also called the spike rush. It has slender, grass-like leaves and has little round fruiting spikes. This is a shade-loving plant. Many water plants do best in full sun, and it is nice that there are some that actually prefer shade. *Eleocharis tuberosa* looks similar but has a tuberous root that is edible. Its common name is Chinese water chestnut.

Juncus effusus, also known as the soft rush, common rush, and green bullrush, has 2- to 5-foot-tall dark green leaves that are hollow spikes. It requires full sun and loam or clay soil. Its cousin, the corkscrew rush, has spikes that grow in attractive spirals. I prefer the spiral variety because it is unusual. Place it in your pond with only an inch or two of water over the top of the pot.

Rushes in the genus *Scirpus* are really hardy and grow like crazy. They make great plant filters because they use up all kinds of nutrients from the water. Any soil will do, and the plant can tolerate some shade. *Scirpus validus* grows to 20 feet tall! *Scirpus tabernaemontani*, also called the zebra rush, has green and white bands on its leaves. If you pick any rushes for your pond, look for the *Scirpus* types because they are especially pretty, can tolerate some shade, and are not as invasive as other types.

Sweet Flag

Sweet flag gets its name from the fragrant smell that is released by crushing the leaves. Try picking off a leaf and crushing it in your hand to release the citrus-like fragrance.

Acorus species, known as sweet flag, come in two types. *Acorus calamus* has grass-like leaves and will have small flowers. It is available in a variegated type that has yellow and green foliage. *Acorus gramineus*, the Japanese sweet flag or dwarf sweet flag, is smaller than the 2- to 4-foot *Acorus calamus*. Plant these in a shallow, wide-mouthed pot. The roots are shallow, and the plant sends out lots of runners along the surface. Sweet flag can tolerate partial shade and requires only an inch or two of water over the surface of the pot.

Part 4

Irises

I am always on the lookout for water garden plants that produce nice flowers. You are probably familiar with the bearded irises grown in many terrestrial gardens. They come in a variety of colors and bloom profusely in the spring. What you may not have know is that there are several types of irises that grow in bogs and even some that grow slightly submerged.

Irises are becoming more popular as water garden plants, and more garden stores are offering them for sale now. There are also cultivated varieties for the water garden.

Irises prefer acidic soils and suffer from yellow foliage if the soil is too basic. They have a tuberous rhizome that you can plant 2 to 3 inches below the surface of the soil. They like rich, organic soils. I like to use a mixture that has peat moss in it for irises. The peat makes an acidic mix that irises prefer.

Japanese gardeners have prized the varieties of *Iris ensata*, Japanese iris, for hundreds of years. They are available in white, blue, purple, and pink. They put on their best show of blooms in July. Place these with the top of their pot above the water level. Make sure to use a pot with holes in the bottom so that they will stay moist.

Yellow and blue flag irises are the real swamp irises. The blue flag is a North American native, while the yellow flag is a British import that was brought to the United States and decided to go natural. *Iris pseudacorus*, the yellow flag, is the only yellow water garden iris. Yellow flags bloom in late spring. They

Irises are traditional pond plants and always among the most colorful.

Yellow Leaves

Irises prefer acidic soils and suffer from yellow foliage if the soil is too basic. They have a tuberous rhizome that you can plant 2 to 3 inches below the surface of the soil. They like rich, organic soils. I like to use a mixture that has peat moss in it for irises. The peat makes an acidic mix that irises prefer.

Part 4

Different species of iris grow best at different water depths. Some are strictly terrestrial.

Man-made

Cultivated species are man-made—that is, somebody has selectively bred successive generations of plants to bring out some desirable trait. Often a new color or larger flowers are the desired traits.

like deep water and can be kept with the top of the pot a foot below the surface of the water. The blue flag iris, *Iris versicolor*, is the northern version. It likes a constant level of 2 to 4 inches of water above the pot and is a lovely purple color. It has a southern cousin, *Iris virginica*. My blue flags came from a friend's swampy ditch where they were growing wild. They transplanted well and gave me lots and lots of plants.

The Siberian iris, *Iris laevigata*, is native to Siberia and eastern Asia. Blue, white, and plum varieties are available. These guys like to be wet and can be placed a few inches below the surface of the water. Once in place, they react poorly to being moved, so just leave them be until it is time to repot. Place in full sun for the best show of flowers.

The Louisiana iris comes in many varieties, but two types, *Iris brevicaulis* and *Iris fulva*, are the most common ones available for sale. The Louisiana iris is native to the swamps and marshes of their name state and the Gulf Coast of the United States. They will do well in most regions except the Pacific Northwest, which is too cold. *Iris brevicaulis* are the most hardy and best for northern gardeners. The flower stalk grows 10 to 14 inches tall. Horticulturists have produced many hybrids of the Louisiana iris. They can be found in a wide variety of bloom styles and colors.

Marginal Odds and Ends

There are so many plants that can be grown in or around the pond that it is impossible to

Part 4

cover them all in one chapter. Be my guest and go look in any beautiful pond picture book to make your selections. You can by-pass the bookstore and go for the catalogs, too. Here are just a few that warrant honorable mention.

√ *Saururus cernuus*, commonly known as lizard's tail, has lovely dark green heart-shaped leaves and a spiky white flower that smells nice. It gets its name from the weird gray-green fruits that form on the flower spike after it has bloomed. They will bloom even in heavy shade, so lizard's tail can be grown in most water gardens. Plant in a mix of half sand and half loam and place the top of the pot one to 6 inches below the surface of the water.

√ Pickerel rush or pond weed, *Pontederia cordata*, is an interesting plant with heart-shaped leaves and blue flower spikes. I didn't put this with the other rushes because it just doesn't look like one and really is a much more advanced flowering plant. These are native all over the United States and are very hardy marginals. They can be grown in any depth up to 6 inches below the water surface.

√ Marsh marigold, *Caltha palustris*, has bright yellow flowers that look like buttercups. This is a better plant for shady and northern gardens. They like to go dormant during the heat of the summer. If this happens, you can plant the pot in the ground in a shady place and return it to your pond next spring. When it's in your water garden, place the pot above the level of the water.

√ Spider lilies, *Hymenocallis*, and swamp lily, *Crinum americanum*, are both warmth-loving plants that will

Louisiana irises include many colorful species and cultivars for warm ponds.

Marsh marigold has a beautiful waxy yellow flower sure to attract attention.

The long, drooping petals of swamp lilies go well with their large green leaves.

not be winter-hardy except in the extreme southern United States. They have pretty white flowers that are very exotic looking, with long white spiky petals. They can be over-wintered indoors.

You are the Artist

Think of your water garden as a sculpture. It is the art of adding plants and fish that makes a pleasing whole. You are building a living work of art.

Your selection of plants will serve two purposes: The first is the practical business of providing clean water for the fishes. You should add these plants for the work they do. The second purpose is purely for decoration. You will add these plants just to tickle your fancy.

If you are not careful, your water garden can become a hodgepodge of pots and plants that looks more like a weed patch. Your creative sculpting skills have to come into play. Think about your color palette. If you choose all variegated-leaved plants, you won't have as pleasing a collection. Choose one or two variegated species that will contrast with the mostly green of the other plants. Also, think about the colors of the flowers you choose. Most bloom in variations of white, pink, red, blue, and yellow. Place colors in pleasing combinations so that you can appreciate the blooms of each plant. A pink next to a pink detracts from both plants, but a pink next to a white is a lovely contrast.

Plants allow you to give your pond a distinctive signature.

Part 4

Gone Fishing

It was the fish that got me into the pond hobby. It only takes one look at a show koi to get you pumped up to start digging. There are lots of other nice fish that can be kept in your garden pond, too, and I will go over the good and bad points of the different types of fish. I promise not to be too much of a koi snob.

Most people think of goldfish when they think of pond fish. Goldfish do make good pond fish, but there are goldfish and then there are goldfish. There are common goldfish, like the ones you see as prizes at the fair, which you will now call comets. There are also fancy goldfish and the koi carp. But wait, there's more. You can keep other types of fish in your pond. These include minnows, catfish, sunfish,

Fish are the reason many people build ponds.

Oscars are tropical cichlids that do well in permanently warm ponds.

Rosy red minnows are pretty, hardy, and active, as well as inexpensive.

mosquitofish, and even a few hardy tropical aquarium fish. Though I'll limit my discussions to goldfish and koi, some of these other fish can be brought in pet shops and through catalogs They are covered in many aquarium books, where you can find more information if you want to try your hand with the unusual.

This chapter will get you started on choosing the right fish for you and your pond and help you pick the best specimens. I will consider the beauty of the fish, but also their utility in your pond. Fish have jobs, too, you know.

Looking for Mr. Goodfish

When you are buying fish, inspect them with a critical eye. Pretend they are at the Mr. Fish Universe contest. No, I'm not being sexist by leaving out the Miss Fish pageant, but you don't necessarily want just the prettiest fish. You want the ones that are well-formed prime specimens–the Mr. Universe types. You want to make sure all of the fins are intact and well-proportioned. Check for any sores or other blemishes on the body. The eyes should be clear and the fish should have two of them.

Look at how the fish moves. Is it active and busy? You don't want one that is acting funny. Swirling around and not being able to swim straight are bad signs. Finally, check out the color of the fish. Pick those that are pleasing and bright.

Civilized Fish

You know the law of the jungle: Eat or be eaten. You will probably have some predation in your pond fish, but the good news is that the predators will probably not be the fish themselves. Birds and some mammals will make an occasional meal from your pond fish.

Koi and goldfish do not eat other fish. No matter what anybody tells you, they are scavengers and vegetarians, not hunters. Once upon a time, some genius told me that I needed to provide some feeder fish for my koi. So I went out and bought a couple of dozen feeder minnows. The feeder minnows were totally ignored and became part of my happy pond family. I felt like a dope.

Goldfish, koi, and many of the common pond fish like to stay in close contact with each other. They exhibit what is called schooling or shoaling behavior. The fish stay in large groups because there is safety in numbers. They literally hide in the crowd. Predators are confused by all the fish moving around. Weak and slow fish are the likely ones to get eaten by predators. Survival of the fittest in action.

Rosy Reds

Rosy red minnows (*Pimephales promelas*) are one of my favorite pond fish. They have a lovely pink-orange color and grow to 2 to 3 inches long. Rosy reds are peaceful, can be kept with koi and goldfish, and are a cultivated variety of native minnow.

How Much is That Fishie In the Window?

I have good news and bad news when it comes to the price of your pond fish. The good news is that most fish you will find for sale will be quite reasonable, and some will be downright cheap. The bad news is that for some fish you will need to take out a second mortgage on your house.

Most of you will buy your pond fish at the local aquarium store. You probably won't pay over $10 for most specimens. You can even purchase "feeder" fish for 10 for $1. Please be a little insulted that such fine pond fish are placed in the bargain bin. Feeders are intended as food for snakes, turtles, and other fish. The wise pond-keeper knows that these are diamonds in the rough, and that many so-called

An albino channel catfish. Catfish have big mouths and large appetites.

Part 4

feeder fish are great pond fish. Your local aquarium store will probably also have some fancy goldfish and even a few koi that will be a little more expensive.

Here is the part where you need to sit down. A top-grade, show-quality koi can sell for tens of thousands of dollars. No kidding! I am talking about major green for a single fish. The most expensive show koi will be imported from Japan, exquisitely marked, in perfect form, and as large as 24 inches long. But please don't panic. You will not have to take out a loan to acquire some nice koi. You will be able to buy some nice baby koi, both Japanese and domestic-bred, for much less. The larger the fish and the higher the quality, the higher the price. When it comes to koi, I like to buy little guys and see if they turn out nice. It is fun to watch the patterns and colors grow and change.

If you must have that prize-winning fish, expect to pay a few thousand dollars for it. However, my advice is to be sensible. Your new pond will take some time to be ready for fish. Start with inexpensive fish and learn how to care for them. Koi keeping adds a little more complication to the hobby, especially if you have show fish–you would have an investment to protect. Your first fish should be fun to watch, easy to care for, and a good match for your pond.

Green sailfin mollies are small and respond well to the one inch rule.

Channel Catfish

Channel catfish *(Ictalurus punctatus)* normally are silvery bluish olive but also are available as albinos. They have big mouths and appetites to match. At a foot or more long they are not the safest additions to a goldfish or koi pond.

Matchmaker, Matchmaker

You need to match the fish to the pond. You will be doing the fish harm if you do not place them in a good environment. Some of the fish that you can keep in your pond will get very large. Have you heard that old story about fish only growing as big as the environment allows? Forget it! It's not true. Fish that are destined by genetics to be large will outgrow a habitat that is too small.

Please remember that koi are large fish. It is not at all unusual for the average pond-keeper to raise them to a foot or more in length.

Platies come in a variety of colors, but they will not survive the winter outdoors.

How Much Fish Can You Handle?

I wrote that in a strange way on purpose. You may want to think about how many fish you can keep, but really your pond will have a capacity for fish. It's best to think about fish capacity as a mass of fish. You can make up that mass by keeping a few very large fish or lots of little fish.

The first thing to consider when matching your fish to your pond is that they will grow. Actually, they will grow quickly. When applying any of the capacity rules I will discuss, always consider the adult size of the fish. Don't use the size of the fish as a baby when you decide how many to place in your pond, or you will quickly find that you have too many fish for your pond.

The One Inch Rule

The most common advice on how many fish to keep is one inch of fish per gallon. This is a very basic rule of the aquarium hobby and only applies to small fish that are less than 3 inches long. Not too many pond fish are that size as adults, so this isn't a very good rule for pond-keepers. Not only are most

Keep Them Small

If your pond is small, please keep fish that will stay small. Certain fish that are excellent pond fish get very large, so you will need a large pond to keep them. Even if you buy them as little pups, you will end up with large fish in no time.

Part 4

pond fish longer, but they are also meaty fish. They have thick bodies, unlike many popular aquarium fish that have streamlined bodies. This means your pond fish weigh more than an aquarium fish of the same length. If they weigh more, they make more waste. The number of fish that your pond can handle is really determined by how much fish waste (ammonia) your system can convert quickly to nitrate.

Bullheads are smaller native catfish that do well in ponds but are not colorful.

Calculating Surface Area

The surface area of a rectangle is its length x width. For a circle it is pi (3.14) times the radius squared. If your measurements are in feet, multiply your answer by 144 to get inches.

The Surface Area Rule

Another popular way to estimate how much fish your pond will support is based on their oxygen consumption. Since the surface of your pond is the place where the oxygen enters the pond, this method uses your surface area to estimate how much fish you can keep. This rule is pretty easy, and says that for each inch of fish you need 30 inches of surface area. Thus a full-grown comet goldfish that is 10 inches long will need 300 inches of water surface. That is a square with 17 inches on each side.

It is probably easier to apply this rule the other way around. First, you calculate the surface area of your pond or container. I have a half whiskey barrel container that is 18 inches in diameter. The surface area is about 255 inches. I divide that by 30 (remember, you need 30 inches of surface for each inch of fish) and get 8.5. That means my little container can handle about 8 inches of fish. That could be one goldfish or a few smaller fish. Are you surprised by how few fish you can keep in a small pond? How about a bigger pond? Let's say my pond is a rectangle that is 20 feet long and 15 feet wide. That comes to a whopping 43,200 inches. Now divide by 30, which yields 1,440 inches of fish. Cool! Let's say I want to keep koi that will grow to 24 inches long. This says I can keep 60 of them!

But the surface area rule has a flaw. If I assume this pond is 3 feet deep, the volume of the pond is around

6,700 gallons. That works out to over 100 gallons per fish. That is reasonable. But if the pond were only half that deep, I would have half the volume. That would leave me only around 50 gallons per fish. That is not enough water for a large koi. I just know it.

So we have found the flaw in the surface area rule: It doesn't take into account the depth of the pond. The rule only works if you have a pond 3 feet deep or deeper. If your pond is shallower, you need to make a slight adjustment. If your depth is 1.5 feet (half of 3), divide the number of fish in half. However, if your pond is deeper than 3 feet there's no extra prize. Stay with the rule of 30 inches of surface area for each inch of fish.

Fish Mass

Finally, the mass or weight of fish can be used to determine the number that you can keep. I really don't want to get bogged down with the math here, but remember that mass takes into account the length, height, and width of the fish. However, estimates based on mass suggest a little less water is needed per fish than the surface area method, and that makes me a bit nervous. I think we should be more conservative when it comes to the number of fish that will thrive in a pond. I suggest you stick to the surface area method of determining capacity.

All these methods assume that you have a biological filter that is the right size for your pond. If you have decided to go with no filter, try 120 square inches per fish. Even then, you must have plenty of plants in the pond to keep the water clean.

Tropicals

A few platies, mollies, sword-tails, and catfish may survive well in a pond during the summer and add color to the margins. Most are fin-nippers, however, and will have to be moved indoors during the winter.

Mosquito fish are tiny but aggressive and eat mosquito larvae—and fish eggs.

Black mollies need warm water and lots of soft plants as food.

Swordtails come from Mexico and of course need warm waters.

Quarantine

Once you have your pond established, you will be safest if you keep your new fish in a quarantine tank or pond for a couple of weeks before you add them to the pond. This will protect the fish that are already there from catching any disease that the newcomers may bring along. You will also be able to keep a close eye on your new fish and determine whether they are healthy. Even if they look nice at the store, you never know what hidden problem you may find by careful observation.

Your quarantine system needs to be large enough for whatever fish will be using it. If you are buying koi, consider 100 to 300 gallons as a quarantine tank. You can use a pre-formed pond, a stock tank, or a small liner pond.

Don't forget that you will need a filter for the quarantine pond. Because of filter cycling and possible ammonia spikes, plan on keeping a comet or two in the quarantine pond as permanent residents to feed the filter.

When to Add Fish

Spring and summer are the best times to add new fish to your pond; spring is best of all. This gives your new fish plenty of time to adjust to their new home and to grow fat and healthy before the cold weather sets in.

Pond fish are farmed. That means they are kept at pretty high densities before you bring them home. The farmer will try to maximize the number of fish per tank or pond to increase profits. This is not a bad thing (you want your fish farmer to stay in business), but new fish may be a little stressed from the close quarters. You want to give them time to benefit from your more generous living conditions before they face the winter.

Part 4

Also be careful with the number of fish you add to your pond at one time. You should only add a few fish at a time. If they are large fish, add only one or two. Wait two weeks before adding the next batch. If you add too many fish at one time, you could create an ammonia spike in the pond. You want your biological filter to handle the new load without stressing the fish. The bacteria in the filter need about two weeks to adapt to the new waste load.

Remember that this is a hobby that will be with you for years. There is plenty of time to build your pond. Take your time and be patient, and you will be well rewarded with healthy fish.

Mosquito Fish

These are voracious little fish (genus *Gambusia*) that will quickly rid a pond of mosquito larvae. They are hardy, will over-winter, and give birth to tiny young. They will chase fancy goldfish and nip their fins, however.

Part 4

Goldfish, Bright & Beautiful

Your first pond fish will probably be a goldfish. There is no trick to keeping goldfish. They are very hardy and are ideally suited to life in the garden pond. Goldfish are the easiest of the pond fish to keep. They are very pretty fish and will give you hours of enjoyment. Many of you will add no other fish to your pond. You don't need fancy or exotic fish to have a colorful, moving display. The goldfish is for you.

Goldfish have been kept in garden ponds for hundreds of years. The original wild goldfish, *Carassius auratus*, was probably a dull gray-green fish that was not much to talk about. A wise Chinese must have seen the slight glimmer of orange in one of his fish back in the 10th century. Centuries of

A red and white lionhead goldfish.

Comets and similar common goldfish are colorful, hardy, and inexpensive.

Sarassa Comets

You probably won't find these comets in the feeder bin. They are a white and red version of the standard comet, usually with red on the upper parts and white below. The fins are long and often bicolored as well. My experience with feeder comets is that even if you find an all white or a partially white fish, it will probably turn all red. The sarassa comet will keep its two colors.

selective breeding later, we have more than 100 varieties of the goldfish. Some of them are so different that it is amazing that they are all variations of the same fish–just as a Great Dane and a Dachshund are both dogs. Selective breeding over the ages has brought out some very distinctive traits.

The common goldfish, *Carassius auratus*, is closest to the wild fish that started it all. It grows to 10 inches long, has a sleek body (in goldfish terms), and is a shiny gold-orange color. These fish are active and zippy in the garden pond. They do best at a pH near seven and live well in a broad range of temperatures, but can become stressed when the water is warmer than 78°F. It is not so much the heat that bothers them but the reduced oxygen levels in warm water. As long as their pond doesn't freeze solid, they will survive the winter without problems.

Comets

The goldfish that you are probably most familiar with is the comet goldfish. The comet has lovely long fins and a body that is not as tall as the common goldfish. They are predominantly deep red in color. You will see some that have a little white, but my experience is that they all eventually turn a deep red. As youngsters these fish may not look like much, but a full-grown comet with its long fins flowing behind it is a lovely sight in the pond.

The feeder goldfish that you will see in your local pet shop are probably comets or a mix of common goldfish and comets. I acquired my comets from the feeder fish bin of my local aquarium shop. This is fine, but I have a few suggestions if you buy comets this way.

You will probably notice that there are way too many fish in the feeder fish tank. The water may be cloudy and you may even see quite a few dead fish floating around in there. If the tank looks disgusting, forget about it and go to another store. These poor fish are destined to become somebody's meal, and many places don't take very good care of feeders. Shop around and find the healthiest feeder tank that you can, then choose a dozen or so good specimens. Don't feel shy; make the shopkeeper take out the specific fish that you want. Explain that they are for your pond and you want to pick certain fish. When you get them home, keep them in your quarantine tank for two weeks. They will appreciate the better conditions of your quarantine tank, and they need the time to build up their strength before they go into your pond.

Shubunkins

I think even their name (pronounced shu-BUN-kin) is cool. The shubunkin has a body that is identical to the comet, with long fins and a racy body, but the fish is multicolored with areas of orange, black, and blue on a white background. The colors can appear as patches or as small speckles. The blue color often looks like it is deep within the fish. I have even had a shubunkin or two that had reflective scales.

Common goldfish, comets, and shubunkins are awesome pond fish. They do not consume the pond plants in large quantities. They are colorful and grow large enough to look dramatic. You will not pay a lot for these fish, either. They rate an A+ for all-around great pond fish.

Fancy Goldfish

This is where the goldfish form gets really interesting. Since goldfish are kept in pools and

Shubunkins have many fans.

A black celestial with pompons.

Part 4

A red and white bubble eye. This is not a good pond fish.

Black calico telescopes may suffer in pond situations.

bowls, they are often viewed from above. Body traits that can be viewed from above have therefore long been prized. Fancy goldfish come in many different body shapes and colors. They each have some particular physical trait that has been developed until finally the fish have that trait in a very accentuated form.

The Eyes Have It

One group of fancy goldfish has been bred to have accentuated eyes. These fish look really odd to me, but some people like them a lot.

The celestial was bred so that it is always looking up. (They were bred to gaze upon the emperor of China when he looked down at them.) From the side, they look like they have flip-up headlights. They are also missing the dorsal fin.

Bubble eyes have fluid-filled sacs beneath their eyes. They are available in many colors, but the eye sacs are the feature people really look for. They accentuate the eyes when the fish is viewed from above.

Telescopes have very large eyes that really bulge out of the fish's body. One popular variety is called the panda because it is a white fish with prominent black telescoping eyes.

The black moor is a fish that has slightly telescoped eyes—although I have seen some telescope-eyed black moors where the eyes pop out more than usual. The fish ranges in color from bronze to deep black. They also have a nice double tail. The body is less compact than other forms of fancy goldfish.

Part 4

Caps and Pompons

Fancy features on the heads of the fish are another way to enhance the view from above. These fish were developed to have spectacular head features.

The oranda (pronounced oh-RAN-duh) goldfish has the compact body of other fancy goldfish, but it has a fleshy growth on its head that makes it look like it is wearing a cap. The cap can grow to be quite large and is bumpy and soft. The red-cap oranda is one of the most popular colors for this type of fish, having a bright red "cap" on a pure white fish. The rounder the red spot, the better: A red-headed fish is a symbol of good luck in Japan because it resembles a scared crane with a red spot on the head. Orandas come in several colors. The spot on the head is usually a different color or darker than the body of the fish.

The egg-shaped calico oranda is pretty but may not prosper outdoors.

The pompon goldfish has fleshy growths on each nostril that make it look as if it is sporting two fancy pompons on its face. They also have the oranda cap. I like these best of the fancy goldfish.

The lionhead and ranchu are like orandas without a dorsal fin. It is hard for a novice to differentiate between a lionhead and a ranchu, but lionheads have a larger cap, while ranchu have a rounder body with a back that arches higher than in a lionhead.

Fantails

Fantail goldfish have rounded bodies, but not as severe as the highly specialized fancies that we talked about already. Fantails have a large double tail and come in many colors. The calico–which is white, red, and black–is one of the most popular fantails.

Fancy goldfish varieties are cumulative. This is a black and gold pompon fantail.

Lionheads are interesting, but their egg-shaped bodies are not made for ponds.

Fancy Goldfish and You

Fancy goldfish are very delicate when compared to comets and koi and are best kept at a constant temperature of 74°F. They are much more susceptible to diseases, especially problems with the swim bladder, if they experience wide changes in temperature. They also have a very hard time in water warmer than 78°, when they will have problems getting enough oxygen. Fancy goldfish prefer a pH around 7.2.

Think of these guys as being like a Persian cat or a Pekingese dog. They are genetically very far away from their more sturdy ancestors. They have been bred for such exaggerated traits that there are actually a few problems that can crop up in them and make them less hardy in a large pond.

The fleshy growths on the oranda can cover the eyes. A fancy goldfish's spherical body is not built for speed, so they are an easy mark for a pond predator.

All this does not mean that you cannot enjoy fancy goldfish. They can be put in container gardens for the spring and summer, if you have a nice place to keep them indoors in the winter. You can even move your whole container garden indoors for the winter. Use a grow light over the plants and provide an aquarium heater and a filter for your fancy goldfish. Remember the surface area rule: You will probably be able to accommodate only one or two fancy goldfish in most containers.

Shopping Hints

It can be difficult to find prime goldfish specimens for your pond. I have already talked about the pluses and minuses of using feeder comets. The best thing you can do is shop around.

But can they Make it?

If you live in a warm climate, you can try fancy goldfish in your pond. The fantail and the black moor are the best pond candidates. Many people love these fish so much that they set them up in an aquarium, where they can be admired in the house all year round. They are really lovely and are wonderful aquarium specimens.

Try your local pet stores. You can also get in touch with your local pond club. It is very likely people have baby goldfish that need new homes, even for free.

You can also buy goldfish through specialty dealers and serious hobbyists. You will find the best fish this way. You can find home breeders on the Internet or through clubs that specialize in particular fish. You may also plan to visit a local fish farm. Look in your phone book or on the Internet to find out if this is an option for you. Ask your local pet shop if they can special-order fish for your pond; they may be happy to find the fish you want.

A black veiltail goldfish.

Goldfish Breeding

I want to tell you about the birds and the bees–and the fish. Goldfish can breed when they have reached 4 inches in length. Changes from cool water to warm water put the fish in the mood. New goldfish owners will probably find it a little difficult to differentiate the males from the females, but, in general, male fish have a sleek body and look much thinner than females. A female fish will have a tummy bulge. Over time, you will get the hang of it and be able to tell them apart. Male goldfish develop white bumps on their snout and gill covers at mating time that many new goldfish keepers mistake for disease.

The male fish will chase the female to encourage her to drop her eggs. After she has laid the eggs, the males deposit their milt (sperm) to fertilize the eggs. Goldfish eggs are a light green color and are very sticky. The eggs will cling to the plants and rocks in the pond. Goldfish like to deposit their eggs on bunches of anacharis, foxtail, or even the roots of water hyacinth. The feathery roots and leaves of

Most people would call this black broadtail telescope a black moor.

Part 4

One Fat Little Fish

The first time I saw my goldfish breeding in my pond, I was shocked. I did not know what in the world they were doing! I really never wondered about the gender of my fish until that very first mating day. It was a warm spring day, and something was definitely strange with the comets. There was a gang of fish chasing this poor little fat fish. They were really brutal in their pursuit, and their speed was amazing. They went round and round the pond. The lead fish would even leap from the water to try to escape the mob. Guess what? That poor fat fish was a female goldfish full of eggs.

Growing into Colors

Here is a goldfish fact that caught me off guard at first. Baby goldfish are a dark greenish black. As they grow, they change colors. The first time I realized that I had baby fish in my pond, I was disappointed by all the ugly black fish and gave them away. They probably went on to become lovely pond comets.

these plants help to hide the light green eggs. There will be plenty of critters in your pond, including the goldfish, that will enjoy snacking on the eggs. The color and the stickiness help hide the eggs, so that at least a few will become fish.

Your pond fish will reproduce without your help. I don't see any reason to provide spawning mats or other aids, because if most of the babies survive you will find yourself with an over-crowded pond in no time. In your pond, there will also be cross-breeding, and your pond mutts will not have much value. (I used to have trouble giving mine away.) If you keep only female or only male fish in your pond, you will be able to skip the breeding blues every spring.

Koi—Pond Royalty

I already had a garden pond built and up and running before I saw my first koi. I had purchased a few small koi from my local fish retailer, but I really didn't see a true fancy koi until a month or so later. I met up with some folks starting a pond club and decided that it sounded like fun. The club met at member's homes so we could show off our ponds and fish. The very first pond meeting I went to, there they were. Nothing like the meager carp that were paddling around in my pond, these were show koi, and they were breathtaking.

I never knew such beautiful fish existed! I had seen some large carp, *Cyprinus carpio*, at the local amusement park, but they were black and none too pretty. These koi, though of the same species, were

A milling crowd of colorful koi.

Just for Reference

Just so you'll know, the following are the major koi varieties usually recognized. Many can be distinguished only by experts.

1. Kohaku
2. Taisho Sanke
3. Showa Sanke
4. Utsurimono
5. Bokko
6. Shusui and Asagi
7. Koromo and Goshiki
8. Kawarimono
9. Hikari-Mujomono
10. Hikari-Moyomono
11. Hikari- Utsurimono
12. Tancho
13. Kinginrin
14. Doitsu

Really Big Ponds

In Japan, large koi are kept by koi breeders in earth-bottomed ponds. The stocking rate of these ponds is an amazing 44,000 to 110,000 gallons of water per fish. That should tell you how important lots of clean water is to the health of the fish.

very different. I found myself in a world full of Japanese words used to describe every aspect of the fish. There are words to describe the shape, colors, and lineage of the fish. I have learned much about koi in the years since, but I know I have only touched the tip of the iceberg.

Keeping koi is very serious business for some people. They invest lots of time and money to keep fish that will compete in the show tank. While the hobby is still small compared to showing other pedigreed animals, it is just as serious. Our new pond club had its own little fish show each year. We had great fun choosing the best fish in town.

Don't be put off by all the high-brow koi information out there. Koi are excellent pond fish and are within everybody's budget. It is possible to collect some very nice koi without spending a fortune. There is certainly something to be said for not going nuts over expensive koi. Just imagine coming home and finding a predator snacking on your very expensive fish. Personally, I have yet to spend a lot of money on a koi, but I have had some really nice-looking fish. Their little flaws grow on me and give them a charm and uniqueness that I treasure.

Part 4

Origins of Koi

The proper Japanese name of the colored carp we know as koi is nishikigoi, which means "colored cloth fish." It is the national fish of Japan. The development of koi as ornamental fish only dates back to the mid-1800s. Carp have been kept as food fish for centuries, but it was not until modern times that selecting for certain colors began. In Japan, where the black carp or magoi was kept in the reservoirs that fed rice paddies, the carp was used as a food source. Once in a while a baby fish was hatched that had red or white markings instead of being totally black. As a hobby, the farmers started breeding these colored fish to each other. Over the next 150 years the hobby grew.

Red and white koi, called kohaku, were the first of the colored varieties established. The kohaku was developed by the 1870s, and many more varieties have since been established. A large number of them are modern inventions and date back only to the 1930s. This is because it was nearly impossible to transport a koi alive out of Japan until modern times. Koi are now bred in many parts of the world, but the Japanese koi are still highly prized.

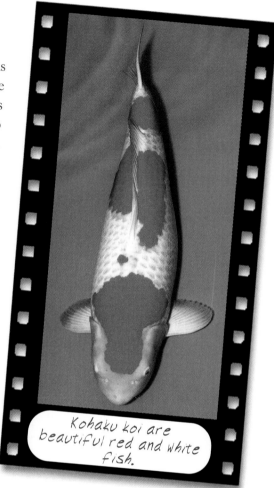

Kohaku koi are beautiful red and white fish.

Float It

No matter how large your koi, make sure it can float in its bag. Think of a beached whale: The damage to the animal just from experiencing full gravity can kill it.

Koi Varieties

Here is where beginning koi keepers get really confused. Koi are known by their Japanese names. There are also additional words used to describe certain aspects of the fish, the color, the scales, the patterns, and the fish's pedigree. It is good to become familiar with the Japanese names if you develop an interest in fancy koi, because you will certainly hear some of these terms when you go fish shopping, and

Part 4

A black and white
(shiro utsuri)
Utsurimono koi.

it will help to know what the heck everyone is talking about. You don't have to know what every term means– you will pick them up over time.

I have seen books that list the koi types by colors, scales, or other methods, but they could also be put in the order you would see them at a koi show. There are 14 classifications for showing koi, and fish are judged with other fish within the same class. The classifications group fish with respect to coloration, pattern, or scale type. Koi are judged by viewing them from above.

This really is a book on garden ponds and not on koi, so it was decided to not go into the 14 major groups of koi and their numerous minor color varieties. Many of the varieties are based on slight changes in size, placement, or shape of a particular spot of color, and the individual fish may change colors and patterns as they grow. The classification is very confusing to beginners, few of these fish are ever available except from specialty breeders or at koi shows, and all react much the same way when placed in a pond.

Also, when you start buying koi you will have to use your own taste and judgment. Your taste will develop and probably change over time. This is another reason I recommend that new koi keepers don't go hog wild and buy all sorts of expensive fish.

You should observe many fish and do lots of reading before buying an expensive fish. I found that it took me years to be able to pick out the better fish in a pool. Save your money until you gain some expertise. If koi appeal to you, do your homework first and read several books on these fish. You will have to familiarize yourself with a very confusing nomenclature and get used to looking at the real details of a fish before deciding if it is worth its price. Fancy koi can be very expensive and frustrating unless you really prepare yourself in advance. It is truly a hobby to itself.

Shopping for Koi

I live in an area where there are not too many pond fish available in the pet stores. These stores have a few koi, but the quality of the fish is very poor. They are fine as beginner fish, but they do not approach the beauty of fish with better pedigrees. Such inexpensive koi may be very colorful and hardy, however, and are a good choice for adding variety to a new pond or stocking if you don't plan on going on to more expensive varieties. Don't ignore them just because they are not pedigreed stock.

You will probably not be able to purchase imported koi at your local pet shop. If Japanese koi are your desire, you will need to buy them from a dealer. Many folks sell koi as a small business, and some of them have direct connections to the fish farms in Japan. You can find listings of koi dealers in koi specialty magazines, club magazines, and at pond and koi shows.

Hikari Utsurimono, here a golden metallic koi.

Lower the Water

The only way I have had any success catching koi is to get the fish into less water. I used to drain my pond to a low level before I could catch the fish. I have also seen ponds where the fish can be herded into a small shallow area and contained before they are caught. You don't need to freak them out; just guide your target into the catching area.

Transporting Koi

The ease of transport depends on the size of the fish and the length of the trip. Most people will transport koi in plastic bags. If the fish is going to be in the bag for more than half a day, add some zeolite chips to the bag or add some Amquel to reduce the ammonia and fill at least a third of the bag with oxygen. Many fish sellers are all set up to package your fish for a long trip.

Part 4

Koi must always be handled gently, so baskets and special nets are needed

If the koi is large, you obviously need a larger bag with more water (it's not rocket science, is it?) and only put one fish in a bag. The bag should have enough water to provide buoyancy for the fish. You don't want the fish to be lying on a solid surface; it should be suspended in the water. The bag also should be large enough to allow you to put plenty of air or oxygen in the bag. Don't suffocate your poor fish.

Large fish can become damaged by being jostled or banged around too hard. Placing the koi in a Styrofoam cooler will help protect the fish, and the darkness of the cooler will also keep it calm. If it is a very hot day, you can place a little ice around the outside of the bag, inside the cooler. For long trips, you can also place some soft packing materials around the bag inside the cooler to further cushion the fish. These fish can be large! Protect your investment.

Handling Koi

You may want to bring your fish to a show or take it out to check its health. Perhaps you are moving fish to a larger pond that you have built, or maybe you're draining your pond for a good cleaning. Catching pond fish can be a huge challenge. I have never had any luck catching koi while the pond was full. I have tried–I really have–but fish are fast. Making stabs at them as they race by has more of a chance of hurting the fish than catching them, anyway. So what can you do?

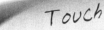

Touch

There is nothing wrong with gently touching or handling your fish if it is in water. Just have wet hands and minimize the contact time.

Obviously, the size of the net should match the size of the fish. My opinion is that you should invest in nets that are meant for ponds or aquarium use. Don't use a net that is for sport fishing. The mesh that makes up the net should not allow the fish's fins, scales, or gills to pass through or become caught. Look for nets with a fine mesh.

Nets for catching koi come in two types. The first type is for

And on the Plus side...

The benefits of going to shows are really for the fish's owner. The show is a fun place to learn more about koi, meet other koi keepers, and watch the judges as they work. Then there is the fame and fortune if you have a show winner. You can win a plaque or trophy and may see a photo of your fish in a magazine. Your fish can progress to a national level show. If your fish does very well at shows, you may be able to sell the fish or its offspring for a high price.

Large koi are hard to hold. The "tail grip" usually works.

catching the koi. It should have a large diameter but be shallow like a bowl. This type of net is meant to gently guide a koi into a water-filled bowl. You want to remove the fish in the bowl. Cover the top of the bowl so that the fish does not flop out onto the ground.

The second type of net can be used to pick up and move a koi. It is called a sock net and is made of a tube of tightly woven cloth. The rim of the net is on one side and the other side is not sewn shut like most nets. To use a sock net, you first catch the fish and let it rest in the shallow net. Then you take the sock net and carefully pass it past the fish's head. Move the net all the way to the end of the fish. You want to grab the open end of the net and hold it tight to prevent the fish from passing right through the net. You can then lift the fish in the net. It will look like a fish resting in a closed hammock. When it's time to release the fish, always pass it through the net and out the other side. You will greatly reduce the risk of injury to the fish by using this method. If you back a fish out of a net, it is possible to catch a fin or gill.

You always want to move a fish from water into water using the net. If you must use your hands on the fish, make sure they are wet, so that you do not damage the slime layer on the

Big female koi almost always win over smaller males

fish. I don't recommend using your hands because it is really hard to hold a wiggly wet fish.

Showing Koi

I don't want to spend too much time on this, but maybe a few of you are interested in entering koi in a show. There are good and bad things about putting your fish in a show. Let's get the bad stuff out of the way first.

There are the dangers of netting and handling the fish. There are the hassles of transporting the fish. Finally, there are the dangers of the show itself. Your fish will be placed in a show pool with other fish in its class. This exposes your fish to all the ponds that the competitors have been in. Therefore, there is a potential to transmit disease to your fish. For the duration of the show, your fish may be exposed to less than great water conditions. The show operators will work very hard to maintain the water quality, but the potential is there to stress your fish. Overall, you are subjecting your fish to a pretty stressful day.

The kohaku (red and white) is the predominant variety that wins grand champion at a show. If you have your sights on grand champion, work with kohaku. Jumbo koi–fish that are over 24 inches long–are also favorites for grand champion. Female fish are favored over male fish because the rounded, full form of the female fish is considered to be much more beautiful.

Breeding Koi

The breeding and rearing of koi in Japan is a painstaking process, and it takes many years before a grand champion fish is produced. The process includes heavy culling of the spawn at several stages in their growth. Inferior fish are humanely killed. This is done to increase the quality of the stock. The less than perfect fish do not even make it to market. When the fish are larger, the superior fish are kept for further growth, and the others are sold while still relatively small. The fish farmer can only support so many large fish, so only the most valuable will be kept.

What about breeding koi in your pond? It is much the same as goldfish breeding. The male koi chase a female to encourage her to release eggs. Natural predators in the pond, including the parents, will reduce the number of eggs. You may find that a few babies will survive into the autumn in your pond, when they may be a few inches long. Just remember to find them new homes so that you do not overload your pond.

Part 4

Look Who Else Moved In

As time goes by in your pond, you will begin to notice different creatures hanging out that you did not put there. A backyard pond will support a whole zoo of different animals, and you will be amazed by some of the things that come to your pond. They will arrive by air or land and, frankly, with some you won't be able to figure out how they got there. I'll bet you didn't even know there were so many interesting animals hanging around your neighborhood! Most of you would never see these critters if it were not for your pond.

The Good, the Bad, and the Ugly

Adding the local wildlife to your pond ecosystem is a good news–bad news kind of thing. Some of the newcomers will be interesting and harmless. The

Skunks are attracted to ponds but seldom cause a major problem, except for smell.

If You Build it, They Will Come

The animals that visit your pond will of course vary with where you live. Possums are a standard almost everywhere, looking for frogs at the edges. Skunks may visit occasionally but seldom stay long-fortunately. Stray dogs may be a local problem, going for swims and even eating the fish. Deer may wander in for a drink and sometimes eat your shrubs. All I can say is, expect the unexpected.

Field Guides

Field guides are books that have pictures and descriptions of the wildlife in your area. You should buy a few, especially those on birds, mammals, reptiles, amphibians, and insects, and use them often.

good guys are the ones that are interesting to look at and don't harm your fish or plants. There are bad guys that may feast on plants or munch up fishes. Finally, there are some that are just darned ugly. Of course, beauty is in the eye of the beholder, but I have yet to see a Toad of the Month calendar.

How should you deal with all the different critters? In most cases, do nothing. They are filling a niche in the ecosystem that needed filling. What about predators? That is an interesting question, and a philosophical one. My main answer is: What can you put up with? More important, what should you put up with? Interesting questions to think about.

I will give you some advice on how to deter or capture and relocate the offending predator. I cannot think of any pesky visitor that I recommend killing, except for insects–which make great fish food. There are some predatory species that are protected and definitely should not be killed, no matter how much you want to be rid of the problem.

Amphibians In Your Pond

Many of the world's amphibians are suffering due to loss of habitat, and in some small way you are doing a service to the amphibians of the world by building a pond. Amphibians live both in water and on land. Some live in the water for a part of their life then hit the beach. Some live a mostly wet life. Amphibians begin life with gills and develop lungs as they become adults. They reproduce by laying eggs, usually in the water.

Salamanders and Newts

Have you ever seen a salamander? If you go out into the woods, carefully lift up the leaf litter, and gently turn over logs or stones, you may just run across one. There are at least 380 species of salamanders (the vast majority found north of the Equator in North America and Asia). Many of them are aquatic, although some live on land. All require moisture to survive, though some have lost their lungs and breathe through the skin, allowing them to spend their entire lives on land. Salamanders are always wet and slimy.

Newts are aquatic members of the salamander group. Their skin is not as slimy as most salamanders and often releases toxins. Males tend to have high tail fins and enlarged hind legs with rough dark brown patches to help hold the slippery female. The red spotted newt (*Notophthalmus viridescens*) is found all over the eastern United States. This newt is unusual in that when its larvae mature they leave the pond and live for a year or two on the land before returning to the pond to breed. They have red spots on a reddish brown to nearly black body that becomes greenish in the adults. Ponds are excellent homes for newts, which will eat many insects—and some fish eggs and fry.

An exceptionally colored *Bufo americanus*, one of the most common toads.

Toads

Toads, genus *Bufo*, are very common almost everywhere, and you probably will see these amphibians in your yard all the time. Now that you have a pond, you will have even more. They sing to attract a mate, like most frogs (toads are just a family of frogs with rough, warty skins).

The toad you see most commonly will depend on where you are. American toads (*Bufo americanus*) are common in the northeastern and central U.S., while Fowler's toads and allies (*Bufo fowleri, B. woodhousi,*

> ### Toad Houses
>
> Toads are bug-eating machines that will help protect your garden for you. You can set out a toad home to attract them. Any container can be used as a toad house; I like to use a clay flower pot. All you have to do is carefully break the pot in half, then lay it on its side on the ground for a new toad home. Some garden centers sell toad pots, too.

Part 4

Warts No, Toxins Yes

The old wives' tale about getting warts from holding a toad is not true. They certainly have bumpy skin, and most have glands that secrete an irritating toxin, so make sure you wash your hands after handling a toad. You will pay if you accidentally wipe your nose, eyes, or mouth with the toxin on your hands. You won't get sick, but you will have a burning sensation if the toxin gets to a mucous membrane. Even the tadpoles may have this toxin—koi eat the tadpoles of frogs but avoid "toadpoles."

Fowler's toad also is common across the eastern U.S.

etc.) are common from New England to Arizona; other species occur abundantly on the West Coast, while Europe and Asia have many species. You will see toads in abundance during breeding season, which can span much of the year depending on where you live. They go to the water for breeding, and you will see their long strings of eggs decorating your pond. The blackish tadpoles that hatch take about six weeks to become toads, when the little toads will leave your pond to begin their adult life. I had so many little toads on my lawn one spring that I could not mow the lawn for several weeks!

Frogs

Regular frogs usually require more moisture than toads. Most look quite a bit different, with smooth, moist skin instead of those oh so attractive warts. Frogs are becoming scarce in parts of the United States and are often among the first animals to suffer when the local ecology becomes unbalanced.

Frogs are pretty loud at night. The smallest are also some of the loudest. Treefrogs (*Hyla*, etc.) are small but have loud calls that range from odd goinks to shrill screeches. They are often called rainfrogs because they call for mates when it is wet and there are plenty of puddles in which to lay eggs.

You may be more familiar with the frogs of the genus *Rana*. The bullfrog (*Rana catesbeiana*) is the largest U.S. frog. Its call is a rolling "baarump." Bullfrogs spend most of their lives in

Part 4

Colorful treefrogs such as green treefrogs will find your pond a great place to breed.

Bullfrogs have an annoying call and also eat small fish if they can catch them.

the water but may sit out on the edge of a pond to warm in the sun. Bullfrogs are voracious carnivores. If it fits in their large mouth, it is food. Fish, other frogs, insects, snakes, turtles, and even birds are potential meals. The tadpoles of bullfrogs are large and can take several seasons to mature into adult frogs. The leopard frog (*Rana pipiens*) is a group term for several similar species of spotted frogs found over much of the U.S. into Mexico. The green frog, *Rana clamitans*, is also very common and is an overall green color in the northern U.S. and bronzy brown and green in the southern states. They have a loud "goink" call.

Tadpoles

Tadpoles are baby frogs (larvae). You will probably have plenty of tadpoles living in your pond. They eat algae, bits of plants, and fish food if they can get it. They also make tasty snacks for your fish. If you keep koi, all but the toad tadpoles will be eaten in no time. Toad babies are small and black. The tadpoles of more typical frogs are usually a soft brown color. Tadpoles are 100 percent aquatic and have gills, the lungs developing as the tad grows. The tail shrinks and legs develop from the leg buds that you can see on the sides of their bodies. Watch carefully and you will be able to see them develop right in your

Part 4

Leopard frogs are nice to see along the edges of the pond and are harmless.

pond, metamorphosing into froglets one to three months (sometimes more) after the eggs are laid.

Reptiles

Turtles

It is unlikely that a turtle will relocate to your garden pond unless you live very close to a lake or a natural pond; they just don't travel very far. I don't recommend that you add a turtle to your garden pond, either. If you really want to keep turtles, they will be fine in a pond; just make sure you know what you are getting into. Turtles eat plants voraciously, and many also eat fish. They will make a nuisance of themselves in no time, munching up water lilies faster than they can grow. Turtles also harbor salmonella bacteria. This is not such a big problem, but you really need to wash up well after handling turtles.

Sliders (*Trachemys*), painted turtles (*Chrysemys*), and redbellies and cooters (*Pseudemys*) are the turtles you are most likely to see basking in the sun in or near a pond. They will find a rock or log above the surface and hang out catching rays. They might even stack up on top of each other when there are more turtles than room on the logs. It looks really funny, like a stack of stones. These are the most abundant turtles in ponds, rivers, and streams in the United States.

In the eastern U.S. you might end up with a common snapping turtle (*Chelydra serpentina*) in your pond. These large-headed, long-tailed, rough-shelled turtles walk long distances overland and move from pond to pond on a regular basis. Snapping turtles will eat fish of all sizes and have a truly nasty bite, so they are seldom welcome in a pond.

Snakes

No yard critter has the ability to freak-out a gardener like a snake. Fortunately, much of this fear is unnecessary. The common water snakes (*Nerodia*) and garter snakes

Basking

Reptiles are ectothermic animals, which means they can't produce heat within their bodies the way mammals can. They need to warm up by basking in the sun before they can get about the business of finding and digesting food.

Thamnophis sirtalis

Nerodia rhombifer

In the northeastern U.S., the common water snake, Nerodia sipedon, is abundant.

(*Thamnophis*) can only catch the weaker and smaller fish, and they only eat what they need–maybe a small fish every few days. I keep minnows in my pond, and I allow snakes to have a home; I can spare a few minnows.

Water snakes are found in most states east of the Rocky Mountains, with about a dozen species in the U.S. If you see a snake in your pond, it is most likely a water snake. Garter snakes are found from coast to coast and usually are relatively slender with three yellowish stripes on the body. They are more terrestrial than water snakes but often feed on tadpoles and small fish at the edges of ponds. Both water snakes and garter snakes are harmless, but they do bite and can draw blood, so they are best left alone. I have only seen small water snakes in my pond, and never more than one at a time. They come out at fish feeding time, floating among the fish pellets and waiting for a hapless minnow to come too close.

The water snakes should not be confused with the cottonmouth or water moccasin (*Agkistrodon piscivorus*), which is found from Dismal Swamp, Virginia, to southern Texas. Cottonmouths are true pit-vipers with a

All the water snakes are harmless, but they can bite if cornered.

Part 4

Cottonmouths, *Agkistrodon piscivorus*, sometimes find their way into ponds.

Learn to recognize and avoid cottonmouths—never fool with them.

deep pit about halfway between the eye and nostril that is a heat sensor helping the snake find warm-blooded prey. You do not want to get close enough to see the pit, because the cottonmouth is very venomous.

Bug Eyes!

There are more species of insects on this planet (perhaps a million, perhaps 3 million) than anything else. They are tough, and they are everywhere, including in your pond. Insects will walk, fly, hop, or whatever it takes to get to your pond. Here are my popular picks for pond bugs.

Water beetles are scavengers and carnivores that usually just cruise around your pond eating litter from the bottom. A few giant diving beetles (*Dytiscus*) are large, voracious, and can catch fish an inch or two long. The larvae are also voracious predators of small animals.

The water striders are true bugs (order Hemiptera) with very long legs that skate around on the surface looking for other small insects to eat. It can literally walk on water because it is so light and has feet that can push against the surface of the water. Other true bugs include the small backswimmers that appear to row across the surface with flattened elongated legs and the predacious bugs with long snouts.

Dragonflies and damselflies (order Odonata) lay their eggs in the water of the pond. The immature stage (called a nymph) looks like a scary water monster. The nymphs eat other pond insects, and they may eat an occasional small fish. You may see a dried husk on your marginal plants where a nymph emerged to become an

The Bad Ones

Gnats, midges, and mosquitoes (all flies, order Diptera) are a nuisance. You know what a pain they can be! They lay their eggs in ponds or even in stagnant water in buckets, tubs, and puddles. You will see a big increase in the number of these guys around your garden unless you keep fish. If a problem persists, try mosquito fish. Almost any chemical treatment may harm your fish.

The claws of a dog can cut your pond liner, and some dogs can catch koi.

adult flier. The adults are really fun to watch as they dart around the pond like little flying machines from a science fiction movie.

Bigger Predators

Predation is a fact of life. The big animals eat the little animals. How bad it gets will largely depend on how many predators are around the neighborhood. I want to tell you here about the bad boys that can take out large koi; some can even wipe out a whole pond. I will also share with you some tips on how to deter large predators.

Cats

The common house cat is a very effective predator of small animals. Rodents, birds, insects, and snakes are likely targets of a cat. Cats will hunt just for the sport of it, even when they are well-fed. If you own a cat, you may have been given the present of a dead mouse on the front step; it's a sign of true feline love. Most cats hate water and will do just about anything to stay out of it. I have heard some people

Cats are more likely to kill frogs and small snakes at your pond than harm the fish.

Part 4

Raccoons are notorious predators on pond fish.

The raccoon is a major host of rabies, so caution is always advisable.

say that cats catch their fish, and it is possible. I am not ruling it out, but before you blame the neighbor's cat, investigate a little more. It's rare for a cat to kill fish.

Raccoons

Raccoons will eat frogs and fish. The raccoon is a very common wild animal to find in most residential areas. The ready supply of garbage has kept the raccoon and many other small mammals living happily in human habitats.

Raccoons are deterred by ponds that are deep and have steep sides. They will not swim or dive for a meal because they will mainly catch animals that they can wade in after and trap. Raccoons also like to wash their meal before they eat it. It is possible that a visiting raccoon is simply washing some food item from your trash can in your pond.

If you have a major raccoon problem in your neighborhood, call you local animal control organization for assistance. They may come out and set traps to catch the raccoons and move them to a more remote location. If you catch a raccoon in the act of raiding your pond, just leave it alone. Raccoons can be infected with rabies.

Great Blue Herons

The great blue heron is the scourge of pond-keepers. Once they find you, these large birds will return to your pond time after time. They are really big birds and look like pterodactyls on the wing. They have very long legs, so they can stand right in the middle of your pond when fishing. Pond fish are easy pickings for the heron. Many pond-keepers report finding the dead bodies of their fish out of the water, neatly speared through the body by herons.

Herons and Egrets

Great blue herons may be the largest species of U.S. heron, but they are far from the only. At least four to eight species of herons occur almost everywhere, and most visit ponds and take the occasional fish. All are large, beautiful birds that are fully protected and cannot be harmed.

Use dogs to scare off great blue herons and other bird predators—don't try to kill them.

The problem with herons is that they are protected by law, so I recommend that you don't kill them. However, there are some things you can do to deter them. Contrary to common information, great blue herons are not especially solitary and are not deterred by a decoy heron; they also generally ignore fake alligators, feeding far enough away to escape if the gator should suddenly come to life. Some people string fishing line in a tight grid all across the top of the pond. The heron cannot walk around the pond freely, and it will leave. A net serves the same purpose. This is not very attractive, and it also is against the law to injure a heron, which could happen when its legs or wings get tangled. Motion sensors attached to a sprinkler so it will come on when a large animal gets within range may work. The sound and spray scare the bad guys away. I like these, and they are now made as a single unit—sensor and sprinkler—for pond-keepers. A dog is probably the most effective method of keeping herons and other predators away. Don't be surprised if the dog winds up going for an occasional swim in the pond!

Part 4

Part Five
Good
Pond-keeping

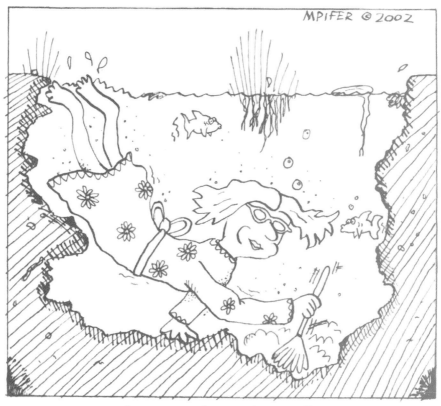

"Cleaning the Garden Pond"

Taking Care of Your Water

Water is amazing stuff! From a chemical point of view, it is a very unique substance. Did you know that it is nearly impossible to make absolutely pure water? It is a great solvent, and there are all sorts of things dissolved in most water. Water is polar–that means that it has an electrical charge that helps it attract other molecules (which is what happens when things dissolve). The electrical charge also creates water's physical properties, such as surface tension.

You probably feel like you are back in science class at this point. All you wanted was a little puddle to make you happy and here is this book full of...STUFF! Well, maybe you have picked up this book because you have had some pond problems. I aim to get you

After cycling, your pond will need little care to keep it beautiful.

going right. Maybe you have picked up this book before you have a pond because you don't want any problems. In that case, you are going to be a very well-informed pondologist.

A Ph.D. In pH

pH is the scale used to measure whether water is acid or base. You read the pH as a number from 1 to 14. The low numbers are acid and the high numbers are base. Seven is neutral. What exactly does that mean?

pH is a measure of the hydrogen ions that are floating around in water. An ion is a charged molecule or atom. In the case of hydrogen (H+), it has a positive charge. That means it would love to snap up an electron (which has a negative charge) from some other chemical. That's a chemical reaction. That is why acids burn your skin–they snatch away all the electrons from your skin and break it down.

Similarly, a basic solution (that's basic as in "the opposite of acidic") does not have many hydrogen ions but sure has plenty of hydroxyl ions (OH-). Hydroxyl atoms like to react, too. They are looking for positive ions to combine with. Drain cleaning chemicals are usually made of lye, sodium hydroxide (NaOH), which is as basic as you can get. Strong bases like lye react with just about everything.

The pH scale is logarithmic. That means that if you go from a pH of 7 to 8, you have actually increased alkalinity tenfold. The main reason you need to know this is because a one-point change in pH can be way more drastic than you think. A single number increase in pH from 7 to 8, for example, means that your water is now 10 times more basic than before.

Fizz

Did you ever mix baking soda with vinegar? That is a classic acid-base reaction and pretty vigorous. The end result of this type of reaction is usually a type of salt and water, not too bad for substances that are so reactive to begin with.

Testing for pH

You can easily test the pH of your water by buying a test kit, which you will definitely find for sale at a pet shop. Most of them have a vial that you fill with water from your pond. You then add a special tablet or a few drops of indicator liquid and wait a little while for a chemical reaction to take place. Your water will take on a color, just like magic. All that is left to do is compare your color with the color chart that came in the kit. You can also find tests that use little strips that you dip in the water. They are OK, but the ones with the vials are more accurate. You can also buy pH test kits that zero in on a certain pH range. Follow the directions on your test kit exactly. Each one works a little differently. Use a good light when comparing your water to the color chart, too.

Neutral pH is usually best for pond fish and plants. Remember, you want a pH of around 7 (a bit more or less will not hurt). Some types of fish prefer water that is not neutral. You will probably not keep these types of fish in your pond. When it comes to your water garden, just remember, Lucky Seven.

> **Caution!**
>
> The pH and hardness of your water may affect the potency of some medications, such as tetracycline and copper compounds.

Changing Your pH

Before you ever fill your pond, you should first check the pH of the water that comes out of your tap. This way you'll know if the water is safe to use. In 99 percent of the cases, the normal pH of your house water is fine for your pond. You should just use your water at the pH of your tap water when you fill your new pond and for any water changes. If you later have a pH problem in your pond, testing your tap water will also tell you if the problem has to be fixed in the pond or before the water gets to the pond. To test, take a jar of water from your tap and shake it up for a few minutes to balance the dissolved gases, then go ahead and test the pH.

I think it is better to fool around with the water only if it is really needed. In the case of water that has a very high pH (over 8) or low pH (below 6), you may need to make some adjustments.

Down You Go

Lowering the pH is usually a difficult task. I tend to be a conservative pond-keeper and try to deal with the natural situation. If the pH is not over 8, I recommend just watching it. If it climbs higher, start looking at your rocks. You may have rocks in your pond that drive the pH up naturally. Soak samples of your rocks overnight in a bucket of water and then test the resultant pH.

> **When to Measure**
>
> The pH of your water garden can vary naturally throughout the day. Nothing is wrong unless the pH is consistently low. Mid-afternoon is the best time to measure the pH.

Many things affect pH, including waste foods and certainly concrete.

Your fish will adapt to your water and have no problems if the pH is somewhere in the 6.5 to 7.5 range. Constantly fiddling with the pH is probably more stressful to fish in the long run than a slightly higher or lower pH. At a high pH (over 8) the ammonia is much more toxic to your fish. When you test for ammonia, test for pH, too! The only time I would worry about a pH that is a little high is when cycling your pond. Dropping the pH to 6.8 can take a lot of stress off fish while the pond cycles.

To lower your pH, make very small adjustments each day and test the water before and after you add chemicals to the pond.

Sodium biphosphate can lower the pH. Use 1 teaspoon per 10 gallons. The phosphates in this salt can cause an algal bloom, so take care. You can also use a commercially available pH-lowering solution that is designed for ponds. Follow the instructions on the label. It will probably have phosphates in it, too, which could lead to algal blooms. Muriatic acid, used for preparing concrete ponds, is a very strong acid and is really too much for minor pH adjustments. Steer clear of it for routine water pH changes.

Raising the pH

In some cases you may have water with a low pH. This is more common when you get your water from a well. Acidic water usually is soft, meaning it lacks minerals and carbonates. You may also find that the pH of the water in your pond may become more acidic over time. This is caused by the natural breakdown of leaves and other organic materials in the water. I think it is a good idea to increase the pH of acidic water to neutral. It is very easy to increase the pH, but make all changes slowly.

If the acidity has developed over time, change your water more often. A 10-percent water change twice a week should help in no time. This is the easiest thing in the world to do. Try adding a little baking soda to your water, no more than one teaspoon for every 10 gallons. Add crushed coral, oyster shells, or other calcareous gravel to your filter box. A net bag is a great way to contain it. You could also sprinkle some into the pond itself, if you don't object to having it in there. The koi will probably munch on it and then spit it back out, which will keep algae from coating it.

Liquid Rocks—Water Hardness

You may be familiar with the idea of hard water because of the deposits you see in your bathtub. Water is an excellent solvent, and your water will have more or less minerals dissolved in it, depending on where you live. You can measure the hardness of your water using kits.

General hardness, which is a measure of calcium and magnesium in the water, is measured on the German scale as degrees of general hardness (dGH or DH). Hardness can also be measured in ppm–parts per million. Some test kits measure it one way, and some test kits measure it another.

Water softener salt may not have just sodium chloride in it. Some brands have additional chemicals added, so do not put it in your pond. If you have a water softener unit, the best thing to do is try to bypass the softener when you use water for the pond. It is better to use water with minerals already there for your pond, rather than trying to add the minerals later. Fish and plants will benefit from the minerals. Also, the sodium from the softener is very hard on aquatic plants, inhibiting their growth and even killing them.

Carbonate Hardness

There are two types of water hardness. I've already talked about general hardness. The second type is carbonate hardness. It is better to think of this as alkalinity, or acid neutralizing hardness. You are probably familiar with the acid neutralizing properties of bicarbonates such as baking soda; most antacids are carbonates.

Carbonate hardness is a measure of the ability of your water to buffer or stabilize itself when there are substances

How Hard is Hard?

You commonly will see hardness expressed in milligrams per Liter (mg/L) and in degrees of hardness (DH) (an old measurement). 1 DH is about 17 mg/L on most scales.

Soft water:	0-17 mg/L	0-1 grams
Slightly hard:	17-60 mg/L	1-3.5 grams
Moderately hard:	60-120 mg/L	3.5-7 grams
Hard water:	120-180 mg/L	7-10.5 grams
Very hard:	over 180 mg/L	over 10.5 grams

Heat Stress

Cold water holds more oxygen than warm water, so in the summer when the water gets warm, your fish may exhibit signs of stress from lack of oxygen. Provide extra aeration to help them through the hot days.

that change the pH of the water. The presence of carbonate and bicarbonate ions can counteract sudden changes in pH. However, carbonates will also keep the pH on the high side if they are very abundant.

You can test for carbonate hardness in your water with test kits that may express the results in the German hardness scale (dKH or KH), in metric units of milliequivalents per liter (abbreviated meq/L), or the English scale of parts per million (expressed as ppm $CaCO_3$–$CaCO_3$ is calcium carbonate). If you have to convert, just remember that 1 dKH unit is 17.8ppm or 0.36meq/L.

Carbonate Hardness and Your Water Garden

If your water has a naturally low carbonate hardness, your pond may have trouble staying at a stable pH. You should and can easily remedy the situation. The cure is exactly the same as for low pH, because the calcareous gravels also add carbonate to your water. A little baking soda will work, too.

I've Got Gas

There will also be dissolved gases in your pond that are the by-products of the respiration of both the plants and the fish. It is possible to measure the dissolved oxygen, but it really is not that important. You should observe your fish and make sure that they are not stressed due to lack of oxygen. You will know when they need more oxygen, because they may be hanging out under your waterfall or fountain or gasping at the surface where the water has more dissolved oxygen. Adding a fountain or an airstone can help.

Carbon Dioxide

Carbon dioxide is one of the dissolved gases that will end up in your water, but I want to talk about carbon dioxide (CO_2) as a special case. Carbon dioxide is given off by your fish and by your plants, too. In a pond, this fact can lead to some unexpected problems. The interactions of carbon dioxide and water are pretty complicated. Did you notice how close carbonate (CO_3) and carbon dioxide (CO_2) are, chemically speaking? Carbon dioxide interacts with the carbonate system of your water. The general and carbonate hardness can both be affected by the levels of dissolved CO_2 in the water.

The carbonate system is the most complicated in your pond, so let's just hit some of the highlights.

√ When the water is neutral (pH 7 to 8), dissolved carbon dioxide is mainly converted to bicarbonates.

√ When the water is very alkaline (pH 10), dissolved carbon dioxide is mostly in the form of carbonates.

√ The carbonates can react with calcium and fall out of solution, which will lower the carbonate hardness of the water.

√ Carbon dioxide can lower the pH. This is the most important thing for you to remember. If there is calcium carbonate present, it is dissolved by the more acidic water, and the pH can go back up. It may take a little time, though.

The dissolved CO_2 affects the entire chemical system of the pond water. What does that mean to you, the average pond-keeper? Let's talk about one more topic, then I'll put it all together.

Plant Respiration

Do you remember anything about photosynthesis? Photosynthesis is the process where plants use sunlight and carbon dioxide to make sugar. They give off oxygen when they are using the carbon dioxide. However, the sun only shines for part of the day! If sunlight is the key ingredient of photosynthesis, what do plants do when it is dark?

Answer: They use up oxygen. Whoa! Who knew?

Let's put it all together now. Plants use carbon dioxide in the day and give off oxygen. At night the process is

Aquatic plants produce oxygen during the day but use it at night.

reversed: They use oxygen and give off carbon dioxide. You have a situation at night where both the plants and animals are giving off carbon dioxide.

What this all means is that the pH in your pond can and probably will vary throughout the day. If you measured your pH at several different times during the day and didn't know about this, wouldn't you start to freak out? The pH of your pond will be lower in the early morning. If you measure pH at this time, you will probably be tempted to make unnecessary adjustments. Instead, wait until afternoon to measure the pH and make changes slowly and cautiously. If your water has adequate carbonate hardness, the natural pH swing will be mild and will have no effect on your animals and plants.

Life In the Big City

City water supplies are treated to kill bacteria and other organisms that occur naturally in water but might make people sick. You may remember the outbreak of cryptosporidia (a protozoan) in a Midwestern city a few years back that made many ill and even killed a few people. You definitely want your drinking water to be safe. However, the chemicals that are used to kill the bad guys are also bad for your fish and plants. Most of the disinfectants used are chlorine-based chemicals such as chlorine dioxide, chlorine gas, hypochlorite (bleach), or chloramines. The chlorine level in the water is very low, so it does not hurt you, but there is enough there to harm your animals and plants.

Ouch!

When you go swimming in a chlorinated pool, chances are your eyes will eventually become red and irritated. If you take in a little water through your nose, it may sting or burn. That's what chlorine does to the sensitive membranes of our body. Now imagine you are a fish, passing water through your gills 24 hours a day. Those gills are sensitive and permeable, and you're trying to breathe through them. Imagine what chlorine in the water might feel like going through your gills!

You should use a commercial chlorine remover if you have city water. There are several on the market for use with aquaria and water gardens. Amquel also takes the chlorine out of tap water. Follow the instructions on the product label. If you are doing a water change, just add the correct amount of chlorine remover to your pond and fill with your hose.

Chlorine is not all you need to worry about, though. In some areas the local water supplies have high levels of dissolved organics. Chlorine can combine with these to form carcinogenic substances (trihalomethanes). To prevent that, some municipal water supplies add both chlorine and ammonia to the water. These two

Check the Water Company

But how do you know if you even have chloramines? You can call you local water utility and ask for an analysis of the city water. You will also get interesting information about the properties of your water. If you cannot get an analysis, play it safe and assume that chloramines are there.

combine into new compounds called chloramines. Chloramines also disinfect water, but they don't combine with organic materials.

Your dechlorinating water conditioner will neutralize both chlorine and chloramines. However, when chloramines are neutralized, the ammonia is released, and we know how dangerous ammonia is. Fortunately, good neutralizers also neutralize the ammonia, but not all chlorine removers are created equal. Some of them release the ammonia from chloramines but then do not take care of the ammonia. Read the label and make sure the product is also designed to handle the ammonia output from the chloramines. If you have a well-established pond, chloramines probably will not be a big deal—your biological filtration will quickly neutralize the ammonia. In a new, uncycled pond, though, the ammonia could be especially deadly.

Help! My Water is Brown!

Brown water is usually caused by tannins that have dissolved in the water. Tannins make your tea brown, and they can make your pond water brown, too. Tannins usually come from fallen leaves in the pond. They are not harmful to the plants or fish, but they are just unattractive to most pond-keepers. I usually don't get too worked up about brown water. I do, however, prefer clear water. Otherwise, I can't see the fish.

You can take a few easy steps to clean up brown water. First, look around your pond to see if there are leaves, twigs, or other debris that have entered your pond or stream. Leaves in a stream are constantly being washed by the running water, and the tannins in the leaves dissolve into

Water lilies help shade the pond and prevent algal blooms.

Green water due to algal blooms often is due to excess nutrients.

the water, making it brown. Also check your water plants. Most water plants have a constant cycle of death and new growth. New leaves are always replacing old ones. The old leaves very often drop into the water and begin to decay. Check your plants and trim off the old decaying leaves. Take the dead leaves out of the pond, too.

Once you've cleaned out all the possible sources of tannins, start doing some water changes. You can change 10 percent every two or three days until the water is clear again.

Help! My Water Is Green!

Green pea soup water is the most common water problem in ponds. It is especially common in the spring. Algae are the culprit in this case. Algae are tiny plants, and there are many types of algae. Some are actually welcome inhabitants of your pond. The green pea soup is a single-celled alga that just floats around in the water, and I can't say it's a very welcome hitchhiker.

You can cut down on the sunlight that reaches the algae in your pond by adding more plants that shade the surface of the water. Lily pads cover the surface of the water pretty well; water hyacinths and water lettuce float on the surface and block out light. If you're fighting an algal bloom, you should try to cover about 50 percent of the open water. Flowering plants also provide competition for nutrients, taking it in before the algae can use it. A water garden that is heavily stocked with a balanced variety of plants should out-compete the algae for nutrients and prevent a large bloom. Partial water changes will help, of course.

Algae are Plants, too

Since algae are plants, everything you know about plants goes for algae, too. They need sunlight and nutrients to grow and thrive. Your strategy for dealing with a bloom is to cut them off from the things they need.

Chemicals That Fight Algae

You will see several types of products available to help reduce algal blooms. One type is known as algicides. These are chemicals that kill the algae. The problem with these is that they can also kill the filamentous algae that are good for your pond and may even kill your pond plants. They also only provide temporary relief, because the conditions that caused the algal bloom may still be present. The algicides just delay the day when you'll have to figure out the cause of the real problem. I recommend you pass on these.

Another class of products to help remove algae is the flocculants. They work by getting the algae to stick together in large blobs that sink to the bottom of the pond. I have tried these products, and they do work temporarily. However, they don't kill the algae, and your pump might just break up the clumps all over again, so you definitely need a good solids removal filter to make headway with flocculants. I rate these as a so-so solution to the problem.

Too Blue!

There are algae control products available that are essentially dark blue dyes. The idea is that the dye will absorb all the light the algae would need to grow. Dyes will work, but I think they are just plain ugly. Your water garden will look more like a toilet bowl than a beautiful pond. Natural water is not dark blue—at least not the fake blue of these dyes.

Zap It

I like UV clarifiers. If you have a full-blown bloom, a UV clarifier will probably take care of it in a few days. The UV light can also prevent a bloom from beginning in the first place by killing the algae as soon as they divide. In the spring, you will want to run your UV clarifier constantly to prevent an algal bloom. I found that I could turn mine off once the plants were lush and full, with no further algal outbreaks, and save a little electricity too.

Dead and Dying Algae

An algal bloom does not harm your fish and plants; the fish happily swim around in it. The only potential problem is at night, when the algae may use up the oxygen. If you have a lot of algae, the fish could end up suffocating at night. The problem is compounded in the summer, when the water holds less oxygen anyway because it's warmer. Make sure you have plenty of aeration in your pond, especially when there is an algal bloom.

As the bloom dies off, there will be a lot of waste in your pond as a consequence. Water changes will help. You may also have to wash your particle filter more frequently until the solids are removed. Make an effort to keep up with the waste as the bloom ends, so that you do not have further problems with the dead algae decaying in the water.

Extra aeration may help control bad smells in the pond.

Help! My Water Is Stinky!

You know that smell. It's a sickly, swampy, rotten egg sort of stink. If it is definitely a rotten egg smell, you could have an anaerobic spot (a spot without oxygen) in the pond or filter. If oxygen does not get into the water because the circulation has stopped or there is a dead spot without circulation such as the bottom of a thick pile of mulm, anaerobic bacteria multiply there. These anaerobic bacteria use sulfur as an energy source instead of oxygen, which is why they give off hydrogen sulfide gas. The situation requires immediate action.

If this has happened in your pond, you need to do a large water change NOW. The build-up of hydrogen sulfide gas can quickly kill all your fish. Open your bottom drain to release at least 20 percent of the water–50 percent if you can. Drain and wash down your filters. Keep an eye on the behavior of your fish. If they seem to be gasping for air or spending a lot of time at the surface, or if the water still smells, do another water change in a day or two.

The best prevention is to keep up with your pond maintenance and not let the mulm build up in the bottom of the pond or in the filters. You don't need to find the anaerobic spot, but you do need to keep the water well-oxygenated (and the pond clean) to prevent the anaerobic bacteria from finding a home.

Do Your Chores

Finally, after a lot of hard work, you have a new garden pond. The landscaping is beautiful, the pond is full of water. The waterfall makes a lovely sight and sounds even better. The plants are starting to send up blooms, and the fish look nice playing tag around the lilies. Great job! You probably feel pretty good about your accomplishments. You have sore muscles to prove that you did a lot of hard work, too–all that digging and moving rocks around. It would be nice about now to sit down beside your pond with a tall glass of iced tea and admire your handiwork. Go right ahead. Just don't get too comfortable.

You will need to do a few regular chores to keep everything beautiful and clean. Why bother? Several

A few hours a week will assure your pond remains healthy and beautiful.

reasons. The first is that your fish are counting on you. They are swimming in a closed system. Even with the nitrogen cycle working in your favor, there are some dissolved chemicals that will not be converted. Nitrates, tannins, and even some fish hormones will be in the water. The fish are swimming in their own toilet, as well. It needs to be flushed. Your filter will work well, but it will need a rinse to remove the solids that accumulate.

I find pond chores, on the whole, to be pleasant. I like to garden, and caring for my garden is relaxing and fun for me. I know many people who did not grow up gardening who absolutely hate garden chores...at first. Even these nay-sayers find that they actually relax and feel a sense of accomplishment with gardening. Gardening also provides light exercise that is very good for you. A day of yard chores is just as good for you as time at the gym, and it's a lot less boring.

Low-maintenance Living

Even if it is fun, even if it is nice exercise, you won't want to be working on your water garden for long periods of time. If you set things up right, it shouldn't take too long to do your pond chores. I think the key to a good design is a pond that is as low-maintenance as possible.

A few hours a week will keep your pond in great condition.

Plant Minimals

Aquatic plants are nearly maintenance-free, but they do need some care from time to time. Lilies are constantly growing new leaves to replace the old worn-out leaves. They will look much better if you clip off the dying leaves and flowers. You may wish to fertilize your plants once in a while, as well.

You should have drains in the bottom of the pond, the bottom of all filter boxes, and the bottom of the pool for your waterfall. Install drain pipes and valves that are large enough to drain off your water with a swoosh. Two inches diameter and up is good. You need the right tools for the job. Get a pool skimmer. Things should be easy to reach. In-the-pond filters are fine, but keep them in reach. Better yet, attach a rope that you can haul them up with.

Do Your Chores

I think it is easiest to make a list of chores. You can go through this list every time you are ready to do your pond chores. I will also tell you how often to perform each chore.

Daily Chores

√ Feed the fish (except in the cold months). Remember, don't over-feed.

√ Inspect your fish for any signs of illness. Sores, refusing to eat, and little movement are not good signs.

√ Check your plants. Have any pots fallen over? Set them right. Inspect the leaves for harmful insects. Use your hose to spray them off into the water. More fish food!

√ Remove any dead leaves from your plants.

√ Check your equipment. Is everything running properly?

√ Check your filter. Is it running slowly? Are the filter pads clogged?

√ Take a moment to skim any fallen leaves. It will save you time later.

Weekly Chores

Once a week you will need to devote a little more time to your pond. It won't take too long—about an hour. Start with your daily chores and then go on.

Spray down the leaves of plants to help remove pests.

√ This is a great time to check your water chemistry. Check pH, ammonia, and nitrite.

√ Open your drains to start your water change. Keep the bottom drain open until the bottom of the pond is clear and 10 percent of the pond volume has been drained.

√ With the drains open, hose out your filter boxes until you see no more solids leaving the drain.

√ If you have filter pads, remove them from the filter box and hose the solids out of them.

√ Use your sprayer to hose off the leaves of your marginals and aquatic plants. You can rinse off any insects that may be setting up house-keeping. Spray with enough force to remove insects, but not enough to injure your plants.

√ Use your skimmer net to remove any leaves or dead plants from the bottom of the pond.

√ Put the filter pads back in the filter box.

√ Close your drain valves.

√ Refill your pond. Don't forget to use a good chlorine remover, if needed. Adjust the water chemistry as needed.

Change, Change, Change

One of the chores you will do every week or two is to open up those drains to flush out solids. When you do this, you are already on your way to a water change. You will need to refill the pond anyway, so just let a little more water out and your water change is already half over. Do water changes religiously. There is no other step you can take that will have such a huge impact on your pond.

Why Keep the Water Clean?

Clean water will save you so much trouble later on. Really. You must keep your water clean and keep up with regular partial water changes. It always amazes me how many people disregard this advice–and this is the best advice I can give. Clean water will prevent sick fish, prevent algal outbreaks, and prevent smelly water.

The Importance of Water Changes

In nature, there are very few totally closed bodies of water. There are streams, rivers, and rain to naturally provide fresh water to most water systems. In a pond or aquarium you attempt to create a little slice of the natural world. It still works by the old rules, however: new water is new life.

Just Traces

You already know about the nasty things in water that you remove by changing water. But did you know that when you add water, you are also adding trace minerals to the pond? Plants and fish need many minerals for their optimal health.

Listen to my voice: Water changes are good, water changes are easy, your fish and plants love water changes. I think you are starting to get the idea that I am a big fan of water changes.

Your fish will be, too. My koi always dart in and out of the hose water. Some even jump out to get in the stream. It must feel very good to them.

The Benefits of New Water

Regular partial water changes will have the following benefits for your pond:

√ Dissolved wastes will be removed and diluted.

√ Nitrates will be removed.

√ Depleted minerals will be replaced.

In addition, your fish will have brighter colors and will grow better. I have heard it said that some fish give off hormones that inhibit the growth of other fish. I don't know if it is true, but it may make some sense. If a large male fish can inhibit the size of his rivals, his chances of mating could be increased.

Step by Step

Changing water does not mean just topping up when you notice evaporation. You need to drain some of the water out of the pond. If you have a bottom drain, this is an excellent way to drain the water. A good bottom drain will also take out much of the mulm that has accumulated in your pond.

Then you just refill the pond with fresh water. Don't forget to add a chlorine remover, if needed. Just add it to the pond before you turn on the water. You only need to add enough chlorine remover for the volume of the water change, not the whole pond volume. In other words, if you have a 1,000-gallon pond and you are making a 25-percent water change, you only need to add enough dechlorinator to handle 250 gallons of water.

Taisho Sanke (tri-colored) and other koi need care as the winter comes.

Dissolved Gases In New Water

The new water that you add to the pond, whether it is city water or well water, may not have very much dissolved oxygen in it. If you are doing a large water change and there is not enough oxygen in the water, the fish may become stressed.

You can easily solve this problem by using a sprayer on the end of your hose and aiming the hose up into the air first. As the water travels through the air, it will pick up oxygen. As it falls into your pond, that oxygen will be there for your fish and plants.

You can also shoot the stream of new water into your waterfall or stream. The idea is to get good contact with the air before the water enters the pond.

A Water Changing Schedule

Since I love water changes, I want to say just a few more words on the topic. You should do frequent small water changes. Ten percent every week is fine. It is also all right to wait two weeks, but then you'll need to increase the amount of water changed to 20 percent.

Party Time

I have talked about how to care for everything but the humans. I recommend a large barbecue to celebrate all of the hard work you did to make your pond look so nice. Humans do best when fed things like hamburgers, hot dogs, and other grilled foods. Side items like potato salad, watermelon, three-bean salad, and baked beans are required to complement the grilled foods. Finally, humans must have sweets to end the meal. Cake, toasted marshmallows, and apple pie are all favorite treats.

A kiddie pool is an excellent investment for moving and storing fish and plants.

If you detect a problem with your water quality, you should increase the frequency and quantity of water that you change. Ten percent every day or 20 percent three times a week will get the water back in shape within two weeks.

The Four Seasons

What will you need to do to prepare for seasonal changes? I want to give you some ideas about what time of the year is best for certain tasks. I also want to tell you what to expect in your pond during the year. A really interesting project is to take pictures of your pond at different times during the year. I was looking back at some old photos of my pond, and I was amazed to see how much it really changed during the year.

Hurray for Spring

I chose to start with my favorite season. I look forward to getting outside on the warm days and working on my garden. There are plenty of chores that need your attention in your water garden. The exact date of spring's arrival will depend on your climate. Spring officially begins around March 21, which is the Vernal Equinox. You can start these chores around the end of March or the beginning of April, depending on where you live and how mild the weather is that year.

Spring is the time to check, maintain, or replace your pond equipment

> ### Itty Bitty Fishies
> Now is the time to remove any new fish I find that I don't plan to keep. I am always amazed by the number of babies I find each year. I put them in the quarantine tank and start looking for their next home.

Spring Cleaning

The first thing to do is to give your pond a good spring cleaning. I usually drain the whole pond. I remove all of the potted plants and move them into a temporary pond or buckets of water, then I rinse all the rocks in the pond. Make sure all dirt, muck, dead plants, and leaves that may have accumulated over the winter are taken out. You should get to spring cleaning before the plants have any real growth on them. You want the plants to be as close to dormant as possible.

I also remove all of the fish at this time and put them in a kiddie pool. I like the small kiddie pools that fold up but have sides about 18 inches high. I don't waste time chasing the fish around to catch and remove them; I just empty the pond until they are easy to move with a net. The water level in the pond has to be pretty low before I can catch the fish. This gives you a very good chance to get a good look at your fish, and you can see if there are any diseases or injuries that need your attention. I remove any sick fish to the quarantine tank.

Equipment

The filter, pump, and UV clarifier have not been running over the winter, so while the pond is empty, it's a great time to do any required maintenance. Lubricate the pump if needed and make sure it is in perfect working order.

Your UV clarifier should be thoroughly cleaned. The quartz glass may be a little slimy, so give it a good cleaning to remove any gook. The lamp may need to be replaced. Even if it comes on, the power of a UV lamp degrades over time. You probably should replace the bulb every two years.

Inspect the piping and valves for any cracks or leaks and make repairs as needed. If you want to make any changes to the pond's layout or add a new waterfall, now is the time to do the project.

Fish Tonic

After the spring cleaning, refill the pond and put your fish back in. I do a salt treatment on the fish at this time, adding one pound of salt per 100 gallons of water each day for three days. I leave the salt in the pond for 14 days. Remember to leave the plants out while there is salt in the pond.

Your fish will be at their weakest this time of year. They have been cold and have had no food all winter. The salt treatment protects the fish a little from the nitrogen cycle, which is gearing up again. The salt also kills many parasites that could be hanging around in the water.

Remember to feed the fish lightly in the spring. Cheerios, frozen peas, and spirulina flakes are good choices. You don't want the fish to start making too much ammonia, which the filter is not yet ready to handle. The fish are also not ready for a big meal. Oh, they may beg for one, but it is not good for them.

Plant Your Plants

You will have your plants out of the pond because of spring cleaning and the salt treatment. Spring is also the best time to divide your plants and repot them. This is a great time to add new plants, too.

Summer

Summer is the season for you to enjoy your water garden. Your job now is to keep things humming along smoothly. You should have your pump running full time, and you may also have turned on the UV clarifier to knock down any free algae.

The Fish of Summer

Your fish are now at their most active. They forage for

Duckweed

Duckweed may try to take over your pond in the spring. The best thing to do is scoop as much out as possible; the other plants should be able to starve it out. Water changes also reduce the nutrients that the stuff is feeding on. You are doing a weekly water change, right?

Building a deck onto your pond will allow you to enjoy it more in the summer.

Some native fish, such as green sunfish, will survive the winter outdoors.

bugs and munch the other goodies you feed them. They should now be fed a good quality pond fish food, along with vegetables and some citrus fruits. They will also be putting out the most waste of the year, so your filter needs to be working well. The fish may become stressed from low oxygen in the warm water, but you know how to help them out with partial water changes. Just keep a good eye on your fish, and check for any signs of illness.

Plants Go Nuts

The plants are growing fast now. You will need to trim off the old leaves to make room for the new ones. If the plants are climbing out of the pots, you can divide them in the summer. Water hyacinths, duckweed, and other floating plants are probably taking over. Just get tough and remove the ones you don't want. Maybe you have other pond friends who would like some plants.

Slowing Down as Fall Arrives

The days are growing shorter and the nights are getting colder. Winter is on its way, and you will see that your pond life is slowing down in preparation. As much organic debris as possible (such as leaves and mulm) should be removed from the pond before the winter begins. Use your pool skimmer to remove leaves from the surface and the bottom of the pond.

Some people stretch a plastic net over the pond to catch the leaves as they fall. Home improvement stores sell this and call it bird netting because it's used to keep birds out of fruit trees.

Plant Prep

Your plants will stop blooming and set seeds. I usually pinch the dead blossoms off my plants to keep them blooming longer (dead-heading). Water lily flowers drop below the surface after they finish blooming; you may have missed a few, and now they are maturing their seeds. The lotus plant has an interesting seed pod; you may want to just let your lotus go to seed. The pods make nice additions to dried or fresh flower arrangements.

Remove the dead and dying leaves as needed. In late fall you will need to prepare your plants for the winter. For hardy water lilies you can just leave them in the pond. You should protect your lotus pot from freezing solid in the winter. I usually drop the pot into the bottom of the pond, but you can also place the pot in a place where it can be cold but not freeze. Your climate will determine how you do that.

Tropical plants should be brought in if you plan to keep them for next season. Water hyacinth will not survive outdoors except in the Deep South, but you can try to keep it indoors. You will have to be very persistent to keep it going indoors, because it needs a lot of light.

Iris pots can be sunk into the ground and well mulched. They should not stay in the pond where the rhizome can freeze. A winter of terrestrial life is best.

Fish Prep

Your fish will start to slow down as the water grows colder. You should now start to feed them light foods again. Stop feeding when the temperature is 55°F or lower. Autumn often has a sporadic warm day, but don't be tempted to feed the fish on these days. It will probably be cold in another few days, and you will load their guts with food that can putrefy and make them sick.

Winter is the resting period for a pond, especially in cold climates.

Off With the Pump!
You can shut off the pump when the daytime temperature of the pond is always 50°F or less. The bacteria that make the filter effective go dormant below 50°, and since the fish are not eating, they will not be producing waste that needs to be filtered.

Fall is not a good time to add new fish to your pond because the newcomer will not have enough time to acclimate to your pond before the winter sets in. Perhaps if the fish has been in a local pond, you could get away with it, but it is far better to wait.

Part 5

Fish like to have places to hide. They will need that even more now that the plant cover is going away. Pieces of PVC pipe or large flower pots turned on their side work well.

The Long Winter's Nap

Well, it had to happen–unless you live in the Deep South. Winter. Yuck! Perhaps some of you enjoy the snow and cold. You will have time off from pond chores for winter fun, but there are some winter conditions that will require your attention.

Equipment

Depending on your climate, you will have to make some decisions about how to protect your equipment from the winter freeze. If you have a cold and frozen winter, you do not want the pump and piping to be full of water when the cold hits. You probably already know that when water freezes, it expands. The expansion could crack piping and the insides of the pump.

There are a couple of ways to isolate your plumbing from the pond. You can drain the pond to the point where you can take off the pump inlet and plug the inlet pipe. Refill the pond, of course. You can then go ahead and drain the piping. If you have a submerged pump, remove it from the pond and disconnect it from the outlet piping. The piping will now drain back into the pond.

Many people debate whether they should run their pump during the winter. People have noticed that if they keep the water moving, the top of the pond will not freeze-over. This may be true, but it is not a good thing to do anyway. Here's why:

Do You Want a Cover?

What about covering the pond? In general, you don't want to seal the surface of the pond away from the air. The fish are still breathing in the water, and you want the oxygen to get in the water and the carbon dioxide (from fish exhalations) to get out. This all takes place at the surface, and a plastic cover over the water or ice will prevent this from happening. The fish will suffocate if the surface is blocked. I have seen people build a frame and cover it with plastic, then place it over the pond. This looks something like a homemade greenhouse put over the pond, and it doesn't cover the water.

In the winter, the water at the bottom will be warmer that the water at the surface. The bottom is insulated and the surface water is cooled by the cold air. Your fish will naturally seek the warm layer for their winter nap. If you use a pump in the winter, the temperature of the water will be more uniform. It was also be closer to air temperature–much colder. This is really hard on the fish. Running your pump just runs up your electric bill and cools your fish down.

Ice

Your climate will also determine how long your pond will be covered with ice. You absolutely do not want the water to freeze solid. The pond must be over 18 inches deep in most parts of the U.S. to avoid freezing. A layer of ice on the pond blocks off the surface of the water from the air, so the exchange of oxygen cannot take place. A hole should be kept in the ice at all times. Here are a few tricks to help you keep the ice open.

A photo record of your pond will let you see the changes that happen over the years.

Use a hot tea kettle placed on the ice to open a hole. Don't lose your kettle in the pond.

Use a stock tank heater to keep a hole open. These are designed to float and use about as much electricity as a light bulb. Keep these away from your liner so that you don't accidentally melt or burn the liner.

Let a crust of ice form on the pond, then drain it slightly. This forms a cushion of air for gas exchange between the ice and the water. The ice layer insulates the water below, so a second ice layer will not form.

How to Keep Fish Over the Winter

If you live in a very cold climate, you may not be able to keep your fish outdoors for the winter season. You have two options. First, you can buy a heater and keep your pond water at a constant 50°F all winter. Your second option is to bring the fish indoors for the winter.

Echinodorus and other tropical plants should come inside during the winter.

It is common practice in the United Kingdom to design garden ponds with winter heating. Installing a heater is relatively straightforward, and several companies make heaters specifically for fish ponds. You will certainly pay a higher electricity bill all winter. Also, I think it is important to set the heat to 50°F and no higher. The theory is that koi actually benefit from a season at the cooler temperature.

Remember that if you're keeping tropical fish, you must move them inside as soon as the temperature starts to drop. Even a pond heater will not keep your outdoor pond warm enough for your tropical fish.

Your other option, bringing the fish indoors, also brings its own challenges. First of all, you're going to have to buy an aquarium setup. If your fish are large (such as koi), even a large aquarium will not be big enough. People who bring their large fish indoors usually set up a pond in their basement or garage where the temperature will not drop to freezing levels. In most cases, an indoor setup will have much less water than your main pond. You can pull this off, but it takes a large biofilter and diligent monitoring of your water quality. There is the potential to lose all of your fish very quickly if the nitrogen cycle runs amok.

Keeping Tropical Plants Over the Winter

Tropical pond plants will not survive the winter season outdoors, but it is possible to nurse them indoors through the winter. You can try placing your water hyacinth in a bucket of water and moving it to a greenhouse. Since most of us don't have a greenhouse, it is a challenge to keep the plants under enough light to get them through the winter. You can place a bucket of the plants in a sunny window and under a grow light. You may also try to keep them in an aquarium, if you already have a planted tank set up with enough light. Personally, I have tried and had no luck over-wintering water hyacinths. The only friends who have made it have a greenhouse. Even then, the plants were pretty ugly come spring, though after a few weeks in the pond they were back full force. Of course, you can always just buy new ones in the spring.

You can also keep your tropical water lily indoors over the winter. One way is to keep the plant in a bucket under a grow light, as with the hyacinth. The second method is to trim off all of the leaves from the plant and dig the root system out of the pot. Rinse off the potting soil, then place the root in a plastic bag full of damp sand. The bag should be stored in a cool place, like the garage or basement. When spring arrives, repot the lily and place it back into the pond. Tropical lilies should not go back to the pond until the daytime water temperature is 70°F.

Final Words

Well, there you have it. One whole year with your garden pond. Over the years the garden will evolve into something really special. It will take a while for you to acquire a nice collection of plants and fish, and you will also probably make a few changes here and there. Each year the beauty of your pond will grow and so will your appreciation of it.

Resources

Here is a list of organizations and some companies that I think you will find useful as you delve deeper into your new hobby of pond-keeping. Some can supply you with information, some can supply you with goods for your pond, and many can do both. Don't rule out clubs and other hobby organizations. You can meet many interesting people and learn even more about pond-keeping. Enjoy.

Clubs and Organizations

Associated Koi Clubs of America

The AKCA is devoted to keeping and showing koi. It provides very good pond information and publishes the magazine Koi USA. This is a very good web site. To find a local club, visit the web site for information on over 100 affiliates.

Zen Nihon Arinkai (ZNA) Koi Clubs

This organization is interested in showing koi. A worldwide organization of Japanese origin, it offers a monthly publication, NICHIRIN, in English and Japanese. There are far fewer U.S. chapters than for the AKCA, so the web is the best place to start contact.
http://www.anabuki.co.jp/zna/english/index.html

KOI USA

P. O. Box 469070
Escondido, CA 92046-9547
http://www.akca.org/

International Waterlily and Water Gardening Society (IWGS)

The focus of this group is on growing of water lilies and water plants. It offers a quarterly publication, *Water Garden Journal,* with your membership.
6828 26th St. W.
Bradenton, FL 34207 USA
http://www.iwgs.org

Commercial Organizations

The pond-keeping hobby has grown exponentially since I started in the late 1980's, and there are too many stores and suppliers to mention. The following three are of special note. I urge you to seek out your local suppliers whenever possible.

Aquatic Eco-systems

Here's the place for those hard-to-find items, including fish farming and pond supplies.

1767 Benbow Court

Apopka, FL 32703 USA

http://www.aquaticeco.com

Lilypons Water Gardens

This is one of the best-known growers and offers really fun events at their Maryland and Brookshire, Texas, locations.

6800 Lilypons Road

P. O. Box 10

Buckeystown, Maryland 21717-0010

http://www.lilypons.com

Perry's Water Gardens

Owned by famous water lily breeder and hybridizer Perry Slocum, this company offers outstanding plants and also some pond products.

136 Leatherman Gap Rd.

Franklin, NC 28734

http://www.tcfb.com/perwatg/

Internet Resources

How did we ever function without the Internet? If you are not hooked up at home, your public library probably has free access for you.

PetsForum Group

Here is where to find bulletin boards and article libraries on many pet-related topics. I currently am the moderator on the Aquaria/Fish Forum.

http://petsforum.com/Fishnet/

Usenet groups

These offer lots of pond- and fish-related chat. Groups you may find interesting include:

alt.garden.pond.chat

rec.aquaria.freshwater.goldfish

rec.aquaria.freshwater.plants

rec.ponds

Warning: the Usenet can be wild and woolly even on fish-related topics. It is best to read up on Usenet etiquette before jumping in.

Index

Photo Credits

Dr. Herbert R. Axelrod: 50, 56, 146, 153

Joan Balzarini: 211

R. D. Bartlett: 207, 210

Roger Bennett: 40, 81, 139, 162, 225

Gary Cochran: 150, 235

S. L. Collins: 205

G. Dibley: 212

Guido Dingerkus: 42

N. Fletcher: 63, 75, 126, 236

Dr. David Ford: 80, 106, 220, 241

Dr. Burt Frair: 239

Isabelle Francais: 211, 213

Bill Gately: 152, 177

James Gerholdt: 209

Michael Gilroy: 24, 29, 33, 36, 37, 39, 55, 68, 84, 101, 129, 130, 133, 134, 139, 141, 142, 172, 173, 223, 237

Ray Hunziker: 176

Derek Lambert: 21

Ted Lannan: 23, 43, 111, 114

Guido Lurquin: 112, 121, 125

W. P. Mara: 209

Peter J. Mayne: 206

Anita Nelson: 17, 79, 95, 103, 105, 118, 122, 124, 127, 162, 163

Hugh Nicholas: 73, 147, 193, 198, 200

Aaron Norman: 42, 207

John O'Malley: 178

Robert Pearcy: 212

MP. & C. Piednoir—Aqua Press: 53, 61, 76, 109, 113, 160, 182, 226, 228, 242

D. Rizzo: 20, 169

Fred Rosenzweig: 41, 185, 187, 188, 189, 190, 191

Andre Roth: 46, 48, 181

Rich Sacher: 173